Navigating the Teenage Mind: Understanding and Engaging with Adolescent Behavior

Dhulia Bharat

Published by Dhulia Bharat, 2024.

While every precaution has been taken in the preparation of this book, the publisher assumes no responsibility for errors or omissions, or for damages resulting from the use of the information contained herein.

NAVIGATING THE TEENAGE MIND: UNDERSTANDING AND ENGAGING WITH ADOLESCENT BEHAVIOR

First edition. April 2, 2024.

Copyright © 2024 Dhulia Bharat.

ISBN: 979-8224973644

Written by Dhulia Bharat.

Table of Contents

Chapter 1: Introduction

- DEFINITION OF ADOLESCENCE

Adolescence is a critical period of human development that marks the transition from childhood to adulthood. It is a time of profound physical, psychological, and social changes as individuals navigate the challenges of identity formation, autonomy, and relationship building. The World Health Organization defines adolescence as the period between 10 and 19 years of age, encompassing both early and late adolescence. This definition is consistent with the recognition that adolescence is a dynamic and complex stage of life characterized by rapid growth and maturation in various domains.

Physiologically, adolescence is marked by the onset of puberty, a period of hormonal changes that lead to physical maturation and the development of secondary sexual characteristics. These changes typically begin around the age of 10 for girls and 12 for boys, although individual variations are observed. The physical changes of puberty are accompanied by cognitive and emotional development, as adolescents acquire new skills and capacities for reasoning, problem-solving, and emotion regulation. This period of rapid growth is fueled by changes in the brain, including synaptic pruning and myelination, which support the development of higher-order cognitive functions such as abstract thinking and self-reflection.

Psychologically, adolescence is a time of exploration and experimentation as individuals seek to establish their own identity and autonomy. This process is often marked by a heightened sense of self-consciousness and self-awareness, as adolescents grapple with questions of belonging, purpose, and values. Erik Erikson, a prominent developmental psychologist, proposed that adolescence is a stage of psychosocial development characterized by a conflict between identity versus role confusion. According to Erikson, individuals in adolescence must navigate the tension between exploring different identities and committing to a consistent sense of self.

Socially, adolescence is a period of increasing independence and socialization as individuals form relationships with peers, family, and romantic partners. Peers become increasingly important during adolescence, providing support, validation, and social comparison. Friendships play a crucial role in adolescents' emotional development, providing a sense of belonging, acceptance, and intimacy. At the same time, adolescents may experience conflict with their parents as they assert their autonomy and challenge parental authority. This process of individuation is essential for adolescents to develop a sense of agency and independence. It is a time of growth, exploration, and self-discovery as individuals transition from childhood to adulthood. By understanding the unique challenges and opportunities of adolescence, we can better support young people in navigating this important stage of life. Adolescents are not just "almost adults" or "big children"; they are individuals with their own unique needs, experiences, and perspectives. By recognizing and honoring the complexity of adolescence, we can promote a more inclusive and supportive society for young people as they navigate the challenges and opportunities of this transformative stage of life.

- Importance of understanding adolescent behavior

Understanding adolescent behavior is crucial for parents, educators, and mental health professionals alike. Adolescence is a period of rapid growth and development, both physically and mentally, and it is a time when individuals are particularly susceptible to peer influences and societal pressures. By gaining a deeper understanding of adolescent behavior, we can better support and guide young people through this challenging transition period.

One of the key reasons why it is important to understand adolescent behavior is because it can help us to identify and address potential mental health issues. Adolescence is a time when many mental health disorders first emerge, such as depression, anxiety, and eating disorders. By being able to recognize the signs and symptoms of these conditions, we can intervene early and provide the necessary support and treatment to help young people navigate their way through these challenges. Additionally, understanding adolescent behavior can help us to identify risk factors for mental health issues, such as a history of trauma, family conflict, or substance abuse, allowing us to implement preventative measures to reduce the likelihood of these issues arising in the first place.

Furthermore, understanding adolescent behavior is essential for creating effective and supportive environments that promote healthy development. Adolescents are at a stage in their lives where they are seeking independence and autonomy, while also grappling with their identities and sense of self. By understanding the needs and motivations of adolescents, we can design environments that encourage positive behavior and provide opportunities for growth and exploration. For example, creating safe spaces for open communication and dialogue can help adolescents feel heard and understood, while also fostering positive relationships and connections with others.

In addition, understanding adolescent behavior can help us to promote positive social and emotional development. Adolescence is a time when individuals are learning to navigate complex social dynamics, build relationships, and develop communication skills. By understanding the social and emotional needs of adolescents, we can provide them with the necessary tools and resources to help them navigate these challenges. For example, teaching adolescents effective conflict resolution skills, empathy, and emotional regulation can help them manage their emotions and relationships in a healthy and productive way.

Moreover, understanding adolescent behavior can also help us to address issues related to academic performance and achievement. Adolescents may struggle with school for a variety of reasons, such as learning disabilities, attention issues, or lack of motivation. By understanding the underlying causes of these challenges, we can provide targeted interventions and support to help students succeed academically. For example, providing individualized education plans, academic accommodations, or counseling services can help students overcome barriers to learning and reach their full potential. By gaining insight into the unique needs and challenges of adolescents, we can create environments that promote positive behavior, emotional well-being, and academic success. By recognizing the signs of mental health issues, addressing risk factors, and fostering positive social and emotional development, we can help adolescents navigate the challenges of adolescence and thrive in all aspects of their lives. It is only by truly understanding adolescent behavior that we can provide the necessary support and guidance to help young people reach their full potential.

Chapter 2: The Teenage Brain

- BRAIN DEVELOPMENT during adolescence

Adolescence is a critical period of transition marked by significant changes in brain development. During this stage, the brain undergoes a series of transformations that shape cognitive, emotional, and social functioning. Understanding these changes is essential for parents, educators, and policymakers to support adolescents in navigating the challenges of this developmental stage.

One of the key processes that occur during adolescence is synaptic pruning, which involves the elimination of unnecessary connections between neurons. This process is crucial for streamlining neural pathways and enhancing the efficiency of brain function. As a result of synaptic pruning, the brain becomes more specialized and organized, allowing for more sophisticated cognitive processes such as problem-solving and critical thinking.

Another important aspect of brain development during adolescence is myelination, which is the insulation of neural fibers with a fatty substance called myelin. Myelination plays a critical role in increasing the speed and efficiency of neural communication. This process is particularly pronounced in the prefrontal cortex, the region of the brain responsible for decision-making, impulse control, and self-regulation. As a result of myelination, adolescents are better able to exercise judgment and inhibit inappropriate behaviors.

In addition to changes in brain structure, adolescence is also characterized by changes in brain function. One of the key changes is an increase in the activity of the limbic system, the part of the brain responsible for processing emotions. This heightened activity of the limbic system can lead to increased emotional reactivity and risk-taking behavior in adolescents. At the same time, the prefrontal cortex, which is responsible for regulating emotions and making rational decisions, is still developing, leading to a potential mismatch between emotional and cognitive processing.

Furthermore, adolescence is a period of heightened sensitivity to social and environmental influences. During this stage, the brain is particularly receptive to experiences such as peer interactions, education, and extracurricular activities. These experiences can have a profound impact on brain development and shape the trajectory of cognitive and emotional functioning in adulthood. For example, positive social experiences can promote the development of empathy and social skills, while exposure to stress or trauma can have long-lasting effects on brain structure and function.

It is important to recognize that not all adolescents develop at the same pace or in the same way. Individual differences in genetic makeup, environmental factors, and life experiences can influence the trajectory of brain development during adolescence. Some adolescents may experience early maturation of certain brain regions, while others may lag behind in certain areas. It is crucial to take these individual differences into account when considering interventions or support for adolescents during this critical stage of development. Understanding the intricacies of adolescent brain development is essential for parents, educators, and policymakers to support adolescents in navigating the challenges of this transitional stage. By promoting positive social experiences, providing opportunities for cognitive and emotional growth, and recognizing individual differences, we can help adolescents thrive and reach their full potential during this critical period of development.

- Impact of hormones on behavior

Hormones play a crucial role in regulating various bodily functions, including behavior. These chemical messengers are produced by the endocrine glands and are released into the bloodstream to be carried to various organs and tissues in the body, where they exert their effects. The impact of hormones on behavior is a complex and multifaceted topic that has been the focus of extensive research in the fields of biology, psychology, and neuroscience.

One of the key ways in which hormones influence behavior is through their role in modulating the activity of the brain and nervous system. For example, hormones such as cortisol and adrenaline, which are released in response to stress, can have a marked impact on cognitive function and emotional regulation. Cortisol, often referred to as the "stress hormone," is known to increase alertness and arousal in the short term, but chronic elevation of cortisol levels can lead to impaired memory and concentration, as well as heightened anxiety and depression. Adrenaline, on the other hand, is responsible for the "fight or flight" response and can trigger feelings of fear and aggression in response to perceived threats.

In addition to stress hormones, sex hormones such as estrogen and testosterone also play a significant role in shaping behavior. These hormones are primarily produced by the gonads – the ovaries in females and the testes in males – and are responsible for regulating sexual development and reproduction. However, they also have broader effects on behavior, influencing traits such as aggression, assertiveness, and risk-taking behavior. For example, testosterone is known to be associated with increased aggression and dominance in males, while estrogen is thought to play a role in nurturing and caregiving behaviors in females. These differences in hormone levels between the sexes have been proposed to contribute to the observed gender differences in behavior and personality traits.

There is also evidence to suggest that hormones can influence social behavior and interactions. Oxytocin, often referred to as the "love hormone," is known to play a key role in facilitating bonding and trust between individuals. It is released in response to social cues such as physical touch and eye contact and is thought to promote feelings of empathy and connection. Studies have shown that individuals with higher levels of oxytocin exhibit greater trust and altruism towards others, highlighting the role of this hormone in shaping social relationships and cooperation.

Furthermore, hormones can also impact mood and emotional states. Serotonin, for example, is a neurotransmitter that plays a key role in regulating mood, sleep, and appetite. Imbalances in serotonin levels have been linked to mood disorders such as depression and anxiety, highlighting the crucial role of this hormone in emotional regulation. Similarly, dopamine is another neurotransmitter that plays a role in reward and pleasure seeking behavior. Dysregulation of dopamine levels has been implicated in addiction and impulsive behavior, underscoring the importance of this hormone in shaping human behavior. The intricate interplay between hormones and behavior underscores the complex nature of human biology and psychology, highlighting the need for a multidisciplinary approach to studying the impact of hormones on behavior. By gaining a better understanding of how hormones influence behavior, researchers can potentially develop targeted interventions and treatments for a variety of behavioral and mental health disorders. The study of hormones and behavior is a rich and evolving field that holds great promise for advancing our understanding of human nature and promoting well-being and mental health.

- Decision-making and risk-taking behavior

Decision-making and risk-taking behavior are complex processes that play a crucial role in various aspects of our lives, from everyday choices to major life decisions. Understanding the factors that influence these behaviors can provide important insights into how individuals can make better decisions and manage risk more effectively.

One key aspect of decision-making is the interplay between cognitive processes and emotions. Research has shown that emotions can significantly influence our decision-making, often leading us to take risks or make choices that may not be in our best interests. For example, when faced with a potential loss, individuals may be more likely to take risks in order to avoid the negative emotions associated with that loss. On the other hand, positive emotions can lead us to make decisions that are more optimistic and hopeful, even in the face of potential risks.

Another important factor that can influence decision-making and risk-taking behavior is the individual's level of self-control. Studies have shown that individuals with higher levels of self-control are better able to resist temptations and make more rational decisions, even in the face of potential risks. This ability to regulate one's impulses and emotions can be a key factor in determining whether an individual engages in risky behavior or makes more cautious choices.

Social influences also play a significant role in decision-making and risk-taking behavior. Individuals are often influenced by the attitudes and behaviors of those around them, whether it be friends, family, or colleagues. Peer pressure can play a significant role in pushing individuals to take risks or make decisions that they may not otherwise make on their own. Additionally, social norms and expectations can shape our decisions and behaviors, leading us to conform to certain patterns of behavior even if they may not align with our own values or preferences.

Cognitive biases and heuristics can also impact decision-making and risk-taking behavior. These mental shortcuts and biases can lead us to make decisions that are not always rational or in our best interests. For example, individuals may be susceptible to the confirmation bias, where they seek out information that confirms their preexisting beliefs and ignore information that contradicts them. This can lead to poor decision-making and increased risk-taking behavior.

Recognizing the various factors that influence decision-making and risk-taking behavior is crucial for developing strategies to improve these processes. By understanding how emotions, self-control, social influences, and cognitive biases can impact our decisions, individuals can work to mitigate these influences and make more sound choices. Developing skills in emotional regulation, critical thinking, and problem-solving can help individuals make more rational decisions and manage risks more effectively. By understanding these influences and developing strategies to mitigate their impact, individuals can make better decisions and manage risks more effectively. By fostering skills in emotional regulation, critical thinking, and problem-solving, individuals can empower themselves to make sound choices and navigate the complexities of decision-making with confidence.

Chapter 3: Social and Emotional Development

- PEER RELATIONSHIPS and social influences

Peer relationships and social influences play a significant role in shaping an individual's behavior, attitudes, and beliefs. These interactions with peers can have both positive and negative effects on a person's development and overall well-being. As humans, we are social beings and naturally seek connection and belonging with others. This desire for social interaction begins in childhood and continues throughout our lives.

During childhood, peer relationships are crucial for social and emotional development. Children learn important social skills such as cooperation, empathy, and conflict resolution through interactions with their peers. These relationships also provide a sense of belonging and acceptance, which is essential for healthy psychological development. Children who have strong and positive peer relationships are more likely to have higher self-esteem and better mental health outcomes.

As individuals move into adolescence and young adulthood, peer relationships become even more influential. During this time, peer groups become more important as individuals start to establish their own identity and values. Social influences from peers can impact behaviors such as decision-making, risk-taking, and adherence to social norms. Adolescents may feel pressure to conform to their peer group's values and behaviors, which can sometimes lead to negative outcomes such as substance abuse or delinquent behavior.

However, peer relationships can also have positive influences on individuals during adolescence. Positive peer relationships can provide emotional support, encouragement, and a sense of belonging. Friends can serve as a source of guidance and advice, helping individuals navigate the challenges of adolescence. Positive peer relationships can also promote healthy behaviors such as physical activity, academic achievement, and prosocial behavior.

In adulthood, peer relationships continue to play a vital role in shaping individuals' attitudes and behaviors. Adults rely on their peers for emotional support, companionship, and shared experiences. Social influences from peers can impact career choices, lifestyle decisions, and personal relationships. Adults may seek out peer groups that share their values and interests, providing a sense of connection and camaraderie.

It is important to recognize the power of peer relationships and social influences in shaping individuals' lives. Parents, educators, and mental health professionals must be mindful of the impact that peers can have on an individual's development and well-being. Encouraging positive peer relationships, teaching healthy social skills, and fostering a sense of belonging can help individuals navigate the challenges of peer interactions. These interactions with peers can have profound effects on individuals' attitudes, behaviors, and beliefs. Positive peer relationships can provide emotional support, encouragement, and a sense of belonging, while negative peer influences can lead to risky behaviors and negative outcomes. It is essential for individuals to cultivate healthy peer relationships and be aware of the influence that peers can have on their lives. By fostering positive peer connections and teaching healthy social skills, individuals can navigate the complexities of peer relationships and thrive in their social interactions.

- **Emotional regulation and coping mechanisms**

Emotional regulation is a crucial aspect of mental health and well-being, as it involves the ability to manage and control one's emotions in a healthy and adaptive way. This process is essential for navigating the complexities of daily life, as emotions can have a significant impact on our thoughts, behaviors, and relationships. Effective emotional regulation allows individuals to respond to stress, conflict, and other challenges in a constructive manner, rather than becoming overwhelmed or reactive.

There are various coping mechanisms that can assist individuals in regulating their emotions and coping with difficulties. These coping mechanisms can be divided into two main categories: problem-focused coping and emotion-focused coping. Problem-focused coping involves actively addressing and resolving the underlying issues that are causing distress, while emotion-focused coping focuses on managing the emotional consequences of these issues.

One common coping mechanism that falls under the category of problem-focused coping is problem-solving. This involves identifying the root causes of a problem, generating possible solutions, and implementing a plan to address the issue. Problem-solving can help individuals regain a sense of control and empowerment, which can be particularly helpful in situations where they feel overwhelmed or helpless.

Another problem-focused coping mechanism is seeking social support. This involves reaching out to friends, family members, or other trusted individuals for emotional support, advice, or assistance. Social support can provide a sense of connection and belonging, as well as practical help in managing stressors or challenges. Research has shown that social support is associated with better mental health outcomes and increased resilience in the face of adversity.

Emotion-focused coping mechanisms, on the other hand, are aimed at managing the emotional distress that comes with difficult situations. These coping strategies can include activities such as relaxation techniques, mindfulness meditation, or expressive writing. These techniques can help individuals regulate their emotions, reduce stress levels, and increase self-awareness.

One commonly used emotion-focused coping mechanism is deep breathing exercises. Deep breathing involves taking slow, deep breaths to activate the body's relaxation response, which can help reduce feelings of anxiety or tension. This simple technique can be practiced anywhere and at any time, making it a convenient and effective way to manage stress and calm the mind.

Mindfulness meditation is another popular emotion-focused coping mechanism that can help individuals become more aware of their thoughts, emotions, and bodily sensations. By practicing mindfulness, individuals can learn to observe their experiences without judgment, allowing them to respond to their emotions in a more constructive and balanced way. Mindfulness meditation has been shown to reduce symptoms of anxiety, depression, and stress, as well as improve overall well-being and emotional regulation.

Expressive writing is a third emotion-focused coping mechanism that involves writing about one's thoughts and feelings in a structured and reflective way. This form of self-expression can help individuals process their emotions, gain insights into their experiences, and find meaning in difficult situations. Research has shown that expressive writing can lead to improvements in mental health, emotional regulation, and coping skills. By learning to regulate their emotions and develop healthy coping strategies, individuals can navigate the challenges of life more effectively and build resilience in the face of adversity. Whether through problem-focused coping strategies like problem-solving and social support, or emotion-focused coping strategies like deep breathing, mindfulness meditation, and expressive writing, individuals have a range of tools at their disposal to manage their emotions and cope with the ups and downs of life. By cultivating these skills and techniques, individuals can enhance their emotional intelligence, strengthen their coping abilities, and improve their overall quality of life.

- Identity formation and self-esteem

Identity formation and self-esteem are two crucial components in the development of an individual's sense of self. These concepts play a significant role in shaping how individuals view themselves and interact with the world around them. Identity formation refers to the process by which individuals come to understand who they are, what they value, and how they fit into society. This process often involves exploring different aspects of one's identity, such as their cultural background, beliefs, and interests, in order to develop a coherent sense of self.

Self-esteem, on the other hand, refers to the overall subjective evaluation of one's worth and value as a person. It is closely linked to identity formation, as individuals who have a strong sense of self and positive self-esteem are more likely to feel confident and secure in their own skin. Conversely, individuals with low self-esteem may struggle to assert themselves and may be more susceptible to negative influences from others.

One of the key factors that influence identity formation and self-esteem is social interaction. From a young age, individuals begin to learn about themselves and their place in the world through interactions with family, friends, and the larger society. These interactions can shape how individuals perceive themselves and develop their sense of identity. Positive feedback and support can help individuals build a strong sense of self and boost their self-esteem, while negative feedback or criticism can have the opposite effect.

Another important factor in identity formation and self-esteem is cultural influences. Different cultures have varying beliefs and values that shape how individuals perceive themselves and their place in society. For example, in some cultures, individualism and self-expression are valued, while in others, collectivism and conformity may be more important. These cultural norms can play a significant role in shaping how individuals develop their identity and self-esteem.

It is also essential to consider the role of personal experiences in identity formation and self-esteem. Traumatic experiences, such as abuse or bullying, can have a significant impact on how individuals view themselves and their worth. These experiences can erode self-esteem and make it difficult for individuals to develop a healthy sense of identity. On the other hand, positive experiences, such as success in academics or personal relationships, can bolster self-esteem and help individuals feel more confident in their abilities. Through social interactions, cultural influences, and personal experiences, individuals come to understand who they are and what they value. By fostering a strong sense of self and positive self-esteem, individuals can lead more fulfilling and authentic lives. It is essential for individuals to be aware of these concepts and actively work towards developing a healthy sense of identity and self-esteem. By doing so, individuals can navigate the challenges of life with confidence and resilience.

Chapter 4: Communication and Relationship Building

- EFFECTIVE COMMUNICATION strategies with teenagers

Effective communication with teenagers is a crucial aspect of building strong and positive relationships with them. As adolescents navigate the challenges of growing up and developing their identity, they rely on communication with adults to guide and support them. However, communicating with teenagers can be challenging, as they are at a stage in their lives where they are asserting their independence and may be reluctant to engage in conversations with adults. In order to establish effective communication with teenagers, it is important to understand their perspective, be empathetic, and employ strategies that promote open and honest dialogue.

One key aspect of effective communication with teenagers is understanding their perspective and recognizing the unique challenges they face. Adolescence is a time of rapid physical, emotional, and cognitive development, and teenagers are often grappling with issues such as peer pressure, academic stress, and identity formation. It is important for adults to approach communication with teenagers with sensitivity and empathy, taking into account the complexities of their experiences and the pressures they may be under. By acknowledging and validating teenagers' feelings and experiences, adults can create a safe and supportive environment for open communication.

Empathy is a crucial component of effective communication with teenagers. Empathy involves understanding and sharing the feelings of another person, and it is essential for building trust and rapport with teenagers. When adults demonstrate empathy towards teenagers, they show that they care about their well-being and are willing to listen and provide support. Empathy can help adults connect with teenagers on a deeper level, fostering understanding and building a foundation for effective communication. By approaching conversations with teenagers with empathy, adults can create a sense of trust and mutual respect, which is essential for facilitating open and honest communication.

In addition to empathy, there are specific strategies that adults can employ to enhance communication with teenagers. One strategy is to actively listen to teenagers and pay attention to their nonverbal cues. Listening is a critical skill that can help adults gain insight into teenagers' thoughts and feelings, and demonstrate that they are interested in what teenagers have to say. By listening attentively and responding thoughtfully, adults can create a space for teenagers to express themselves and feel heard. Additionally, paying attention to teenagers' body language and tone of voice can provide valuable clues about their emotions and help adults respond in a sensitive and supportive manner.

Another important communication strategy with teenagers is to be patient and flexible. Adolescents can be unpredictable and may not always be receptive to engaging in conversations with adults. It is important for adults to approach communication with teenagers with patience and a willingness to adapt to their needs and preferences. Adults should be prepared to initiate conversations at a time when teenagers are most likely to be receptive, and be flexible in their approach to accommodate teenagers' schedules and preferences. By being patient and flexible, adults can create opportunities for meaningful communication with teenagers and build trust and rapport over time.

Furthermore, adults can enhance communication with teenagers by being transparent and honest. Adolescents can often sense when adults are being insincere or withholding information, and this can erode trust and hinder effective communication. It is essential for adults to be honest and transparent in their interactions with teenagers, and to provide clear and accurate information when discussing sensitive topics. By being forthcoming and honest, adults can build credibility and foster open communication with teenagers. Adults should also be prepared to address difficult or uncomfortable topics with teenagers in a sensitive and nonjudgmental manner, and provide guidance and support as needed. By approaching conversations with teenagers with sensitivity and empathy, adults can create a safe and supportive environment for communication. Employing active listening, patience, flexibility, transparency, and honesty can further enhance communication with teenagers and build strong and positive relationships. Ultimately, effective communication with teenagers is about establishing trust, fostering understanding, and providing support as they navigate the challenges of adolescence. By employing these strategies, adults can create opportunities for meaningful communication with teenagers and help them develop the skills and resilience they need to thrive.

- Building trust and rapport

Trust and rapport are essential elements in any relationship, whether it be personal or professional. Building trust and rapport is a process that takes time and effort, but the benefits are invaluable. Trust is the foundation of any successful relationship, and without it, communication and collaboration can become strained. Rapport, on the other hand, is the connection and understanding that exists between individuals, which can help to strengthen trust and build a more positive and productive relationship.

One of the key ways to build trust and rapport is through effective communication. Communication is the cornerstone of any relationship, and it is essential to establish clear and open lines of communication in order to build trust and rapport. This involves active listening, sharing information openly and honestly, and being transparent about your intentions and actions. By communicating effectively, you can show others that you are approachable, trustworthy, and reliable, which can help to foster trust and strengthen the bond between you.

Another important aspect of building trust and rapport is through building credibility and reliability. Credibility refers to the trustworthiness and expertise that others perceive in you, while reliability refers to your ability to deliver on your promises and commitments. By consistently demonstrating credibility and reliability in your actions and behaviors, you can show others that you are dependable, honest, and capable, which can help to build trust and rapport. This can be achieved through delivering on your promises, being consistent in your actions, and demonstrating competence in your role.

Building trust and rapport also involves showing empathy and understanding towards others. Empathy is the ability to put yourself in someone else's shoes and understand their perspective, feelings, and emotions. By demonstrating empathy towards others, you can show that you care about their well-being and are willing to listen and support them. This can help to build trust and rapport by creating a sense of connection and understanding between you and others. By showing empathy and understanding towards others, you can build a more positive and supportive relationship, which can strengthen trust and rapport.

In addition to communication, credibility, reliability, and empathy, building trust and rapport also involves building authenticity and transparency. Authenticity refers to being genuine, honest, and true to yourself, while transparency refers to being open and honest in your communication and actions. By being authentic and transparent, you can show others that you are trustworthy, reliable, and genuine, which can help to build trust and rapport. This involves being open about your thoughts, feelings, and intentions, as well as being genuine in your interactions with others. By being authentic and transparent, you can create a sense of authenticity and honesty in your relationship, which can help to strengthen trust and rapport.

Building trust and rapport is a continuous process that requires effort, patience, and consistency. It is important to be proactive in building trust and rapport, and to continuously work on strengthening the relationship through effective communication, credibility, reliability, empathy, authenticity, and transparency. By demonstrating these qualities and behaviors consistently, you can build a more positive and productive relationship with others, which can help to foster trust and rapport. Trust and rapport are essential elements in any relationship, and by focusing on building and maintaining these qualities, you can create more positive, supportive, and successful relationships in both your personal and professional life.

- Handling conflicts and misunderstandings

Conflict and misunderstandings are common occurrences in both personal and professional relationships. It is important to address these issues promptly and effectively in order to maintain healthy and productive relationships. By addressing conflicts and misunderstandings head-on, individuals can prevent further escalation and work towards finding a resolution that is satisfactory to all parties involved.

When faced with a conflict or misunderstanding, it is important to first acknowledge the issue at hand. This may involve having a conversation with the person(s) involved to express concerns and share perspectives. It is crucial to remain calm and respectful during this conversation in order to create a safe and open environment for communication. By actively listening to the other person's point of view, individuals can gain a better understanding of the situation and work towards finding common ground.

In some cases, conflicts and misunderstandings may be the result of miscommunication or differing interpretations of a situation. By clarifying expectations and ensuring that both parties are on the same page, individuals can prevent future misunderstandings from occurring. Effective communication is key to resolving conflicts and preventing misunderstandings, so it is important to be clear and concise in one's communication.

When addressing conflicts and misunderstandings, it is important to focus on finding a solution that is mutually beneficial to all parties involved. This may require compromise and a willingness to see things from the other person's perspective. By working together to find a solution, individuals can strengthen their relationships and build trust with one another.

It is also important to be mindful of one's emotions and reactions when handling conflicts and misunderstandings. It can be easy to become defensive or emotional during these situations, but it is important to remain calm and composed in order to have a productive conversation. By taking a step back and considering the situation objectively, individuals can approach conflicts and misunderstandings with a clear mind and a positive attitude.

In some cases, it may be helpful to seek the assistance of a neutral third party, such as a mediator or counselor, to help facilitate a resolution. These professionals can provide an outside perspective and help guide the conversation towards a mutually agreeable solution. By involving a third party, individuals can ensure that conflicts and misunderstandings are addressed in a fair and objective manner. By acknowledging the issue, clarifying expectations, and focusing on finding a mutually beneficial solution, individuals can navigate conflicts and misunderstandings with grace and professionalism. It is important to approach these situations with an open mind and a willingness to listen and compromise in order to maintain healthy and productive relationships. 23

Chapter 5: Behavioral Challenges

- COMMON BEHAVIORAL issues in adolescence

Adolescence is a critical period of development characterized by numerous physical, emotional, and cognitive changes. It is during this time that many individuals struggle with common behavioral issues that can significantly impact their overall well-being and future success. Understanding these issues and their underlying causes is crucial for parents, educators, and mental health professionals to provide appropriate support and guidance to adolescents as they navigate this challenging stage of life.

One of the most common behavioral issues observed in adolescents is defiance and rebelliousness. This behavior is often characterized by a persistent refusal to comply with rules and authority figures, as well as a tendency to engage in risky or impulsive behaviors. While some level of defiance is a normal part of adolescent development as individuals assert their independence and identity, excessive or disruptive defiance can indicate underlying issues such as a lack of boundaries, low self-esteem, or a desire for attention. Addressing these issues requires a combination of establishing clear expectations and consequences, fostering open communication, and providing opportunities for adolescents to express themselves in healthy ways.

Another common behavioral issue in adolescence is aggression and hostility. This behavior can manifest in verbal or physical outbursts, bullying, or conflicts with peers and adults. Aggressive behavior is often a response to feelings of anger, frustration, or powerlessness, and may stem from a variety of sources such as familial stress, social pressure, or emotional trauma. Helping adolescents manage their aggression involves teaching them healthy coping strategies, fostering empathy and conflict resolution skills, and addressing any underlying emotional or psychological issues through therapy or counseling.

Substance abuse is another prevalent behavioral issue among adolescents, with many individuals experimenting with drugs and alcohol as a way to cope with stress, peer pressure, or emotional pain. Substance abuse can have serious consequences on an adolescent's physical health, mental well-being, and future prospects, making it essential to address this issue proactively. Educating adolescents about the risks and consequences of substance abuse, promoting healthy coping mechanisms, and providing access to support services such as counseling or rehabilitation programs can help prevent and address substance abuse in adolescents.

Academic issues are also common among adolescents, with many individuals struggling with motivation, concentration, and performance in school. Academic issues can be caused by a variety of factors such as learning disabilities, ADHD, anxiety, or familial stress, and can have a significant impact on an adolescent's self-esteem and future opportunities. Addressing academic issues involves identifying and addressing any underlying learning or emotional difficulties, providing academic support and accommodations as needed, and encouraging adolescents to develop effective study habits and time management skills.

Depression and anxiety are prevalent mental health issues among adolescents, with many individuals experiencing feelings of sadness, anxiety, or hopelessness that interfere with their daily functioning and quality of life. Depression and anxiety can be caused by a combination of genetic, biological, environmental, and psychological factors, and may be exacerbated by stress, trauma, or social isolation. Addressing depression and anxiety in adolescents requires a comprehensive approach that includes therapy, medication, lifestyle changes, and social support to help individuals manage their symptoms and improve their overall well-being. By understanding the underlying causes of these issues and providing appropriate support and guidance, parents, educators, and mental health professionals can help adolescents navigate this critical stage of life with confidence and resilience. Addressing common behavioral issues in adolescence requires a multi-faceted approach that includes establishing clear boundaries and expectations, fostering open communication, promoting healthy coping mechanisms, and providing access to support services as needed. By working together to address these issues proactively, we can help adolescents develop the skills and resilience they need to thrive during this transformative stage of life.

- Strategies for managing and addressing problem behaviors

Problem behaviors can be challenging to manage and address, but with the right strategies in place, they can be effectively addressed and minimized. One key strategy for managing problem behaviors is to identify the root cause of the behavior. By understanding why the behavior is occurring, it becomes easier to address it in a meaningful way. This often involves conducting a functional assessment to determine the antecedents and consequences that are maintaining the behavior. Once the root cause is identified, appropriate interventions can be put in place to address the behavior.

Another important strategy for managing problem behaviors is to establish clear expectations and boundaries. Consistency is key when it comes to addressing problematic behaviors, so it is important to ensure that everyone involved in managing the behavior is on the same page. This includes clearly communicating expectations and consequences, as well as consistently enforcing them. By setting clear boundaries and expectations, individuals are more likely to understand what is expected of them and what will happen if they engage in problem behaviors.

In addition to identifying the root cause and establishing clear expectations, it is also important to use positive reinforcement to encourage positive behaviors. Positive reinforcement involves providing a reward or praise for desired behaviors, which can help to shape and maintain those behaviors over time. By reinforcing positive behaviors, individuals are more likely to engage in them in the future, which can help to reduce problem behaviors. It is important to provide immediate and consistent reinforcement to ensure that the desired behaviors are reinforced effectively.

Another effective strategy for managing problem behaviors is to teach alternative behaviors to replace the problem behavior. It is important to provide individuals with alternative ways to meet their needs or desires in a more appropriate manner. This may involve teaching individuals coping skills, problem-solving strategies, or communication techniques to help them navigate challenging situations. By providing individuals with the tools they need to address their needs in a more adaptive way, problem behaviors are less likely to occur.

Furthermore, it is important to consider the individual's unique needs and characteristics when developing strategies to manage problem behaviors. Every individual is different, and what works for one person may not work for another. It is important to consider factors such as age, developmental level, communication abilities, and any underlying conditions when developing strategies to address problem behaviors. By taking into account the individual's unique needs and characteristics, interventions can be tailored to address the specific challenges they are facing.

Lastly, collaboration and communication are essential when it comes to managing problem behaviors. It is important to foster open communication between all individuals involved in managing the behavior, including family members, caregivers, teachers, and other professionals. By working together and sharing information and insights, it becomes easier to develop a comprehensive plan to address problem behaviors effectively. Collaboration also allows for different perspectives and expertise to be brought to the table, which can lead to more successful outcomes in managing and addressing problem behaviors.

- Support systems and resources for parents and caregivers

Support systems and resources for parents and caregivers play a crucial role in promoting the well-being of families and children. As parenting can be a challenging and overwhelming experience at times, having access to a network of support can help caregivers navigate the various demands of raising children while also taking care of themselves. There are a variety of support systems and resources available to parents and caregivers, including community organizations, online forums, and professional services. By utilizing these resources, parents can receive guidance, information, and emotional support to help them navigate the ups and downs of parenting.

One of the key benefits of support systems for parents and caregivers is the sense of community and connection they provide. Parenting can be an isolating experience, especially for new parents who may feel overwhelmed or unsure of themselves. By joining a support group or community organization, parents can connect with others who are going through similar experiences and share advice, tips, and resources. This sense of camaraderie can help combat feelings of isolation and provide a valuable source of emotional support. Additionally, being part of a support system can help parents build a sense of belonging and community, which can be beneficial for both their own mental health and that of their children.

Support systems and resources for parents and caregivers can also provide valuable information and guidance on various aspects of parenting. From child development milestones to behavior management techniques, parents can benefit from the expertise and knowledge of professionals and experienced caregivers. Parenting workshops, seminars, and online resources offer valuable information on a wide range of parenting topics, including discipline, communication, and self-care. By accessing these resources, parents can gain the tools and strategies they need to navigate the challenges of parenting with confidence and resilience.

In addition to emotional support and practical guidance, support systems for parents and caregivers can also offer access to professional services and resources. This can include mental health services, counseling, and parenting classes. These services can be particularly valuable for parents who are struggling with mental health issues, stress, or challenges in their family life. By seeking help from professionals, parents can receive personalized support and therapy to address their specific needs and concerns. This can help improve their mental health and overall well-being, as well as their ability to care for their children effectively.

Support systems and resources for parents and caregivers can also promote positive parenting practices and healthy family relationships. By participating in parenting programs and workshops, parents can learn effective communication strategies, conflict resolution skills, and positive discipline techniques. These resources can help parents build strong, nurturing relationships with their children based on trust, respect, and understanding. By promoting positive parenting practices, support systems can help foster a healthy family environment where children can thrive and develop to their full potential. By providing emotional support, practical guidance, and access to professional services, these resources can help parents navigate the challenges of parenting with confidence and resilience. Support systems also offer a sense of community and connection, which can help combat feelings of isolation and provide valuable social support. By utilizing these resources, parents and caregivers can build strong, nurturing relationships with their children and create a positive family environment where everyone can thrive.

Chapter 6: Mental Health and Well-being

- UNDERSTANDING MENTAL health issues in teenagers

Mental health is a crucial aspect of overall well-being, and it is especially important to address in teenagers as they navigate the challenges of adolescence. Adolescence is a time of significant physical, emotional, and cognitive changes, and it is not uncommon for teenagers to experience mental health issues during this stage of development. Understanding and addressing mental health issues in teenagers is essential to ensuring their long-term well-being and success.

One of the most common mental health issues that teenagers face is depression. Depression is a mood disorder that can have a profound impact on a teenager's thoughts, feelings, and behaviors. Symptoms of depression can include persistent feelings of sadness or hopelessness, changes in appetite or sleep patterns, loss of interest in activities that were once enjoyable, and difficulty concentrating or making decisions. If left untreated, depression can significantly impair a teenager's ability to function in their daily life and can increase the risk of self-harm or suicide.

Another common mental health issue that teenagers may experience is anxiety. Anxiety is a normal response to stress or danger, but when it becomes excessive or persistent, it can interfere with a teenager's ability to cope with everyday challenges. Symptoms of anxiety can include excessive worry or fear, physical symptoms such as rapid heartbeat or sweating, and avoidance of certain situations or activities. Like depression, untreated anxiety can have a significant impact on a teenager's quality of life and can increase the risk of developing other mental health issues.

In addition to depression and anxiety, teenagers may also experience other mental health issues such as eating disorders, substance abuse, or self-harm. Eating disorders, such as anorexia nervosa or bulimia nervosa, are serious conditions that can have severe physical and psychological consequences. Substance abuse, including alcohol and drug abuse, can also have a significant impact on a teenager's mental health and overall well-being. Self-harm, such as cutting or burning oneself, is a maladaptive coping mechanism that some teenagers may use to deal with emotional pain or stress.

There are many factors that can contribute to the development of mental health issues in teenagers. Biological factors, such as genetics or neurochemical imbalances, can play a role in predisposing a teenager to mental health issues. Environmental factors, such as exposure to trauma, chronic stress, or a lack of social support, can also increase the risk of developing mental health issues. Additionally, teenagers who have a family history of mental health issues or who have experienced significant life changes or challenges may be more vulnerable to developing mental health issues.

It is important to recognize the signs and symptoms of mental health issues in teenagers and to seek help if needed. Parents, teachers, and other trusted adults can play a crucial role in supporting teenagers who may be struggling with mental health issues. Some signs that a teenager may be experiencing a mental health issue include changes in mood or behavior, withdrawal from friends or activities, changes in appetite or sleep patterns, and difficulty concentrating or making decisions. If a teenager is exhibiting these signs, it is important to talk to them about their concerns and to seek help from a mental health professional.

Treatment for mental health issues in teenagers typically involves a combination of psychotherapy, medication, and lifestyle changes. Psychotherapy, such as cognitive-behavioral therapy (CBT) or dialectical behavior therapy (DBT), can help teenagers identify and change maladaptive thoughts and behaviors that contribute to their mental health issues. Medication, such as antidepressants or anti-anxiety medications, may be prescribed to help alleviate symptoms of depression or anxiety. Lifestyle changes, such as regular exercise, healthy eating habits, and stress management techniques, can also play a role in improving a teenager's mental health. Depression, anxiety, eating disorders, substance abuse, and self-harm are common mental health issues that teenagers may experience, and it is important to recognize the signs and symptoms of these issues and seek help if needed. Factors such as genetics, environment, and life experiences can contribute to the development of mental health issues in teenagers, and it is important for parents, teachers, and other trusted adults to provide support and guidance to teenagers who may be struggling with their mental health. Treatment for mental health issues in teenagers typically involves a combination of psychotherapy, medication, and lifestyle changes, and early intervention is key to promoting positive outcomes for teenagers with mental health issues. By understanding and addressing mental health issues in teenagers, we can help them navigate the challenges of adolescence and achieve optimal mental health and well-being.

- Signs and symptoms of common disorders

Signs and symptoms of common disorders are important to recognize and understand in order to provide proper care and treatment for individuals who may be suffering from these conditions.

One such common disorder is depression, which is characterized by persistent feelings of sadness, hopelessness, and loss of interest in activities that were once enjoyable. Other symptoms of depression may include changes in sleep patterns, appetite, and weight, as well as fatigue, irritability, and difficulty concentrating.

Anxiety disorders are another common type of mental health condition that can manifest in various ways. Generalized anxiety disorder involves excessive worry and anxiety about a wide range of events or activities, while panic disorder is characterized by sudden and intense episodes of fear or unease, often accompanied by physical symptoms such as chest pain, palpitations, and shortness of breath. Phobias are another type of anxiety disorder that involve an extreme and irrational fear of a specific object or situation, such as heights, animals, or social interactions.

Bipolar disorder is a mood disorder that involves alternating episodes of mania and depression. During a manic episode, individuals may experience elevated mood, increased energy, and impulsive behavior, while depressive episodes are characterized by persistent feelings of sadness, guilt, and hopelessness. Other symptoms of bipolar disorder may include changes in sleep patterns, appetite, and weight, as well as difficulty concentrating and making decisions.

Schizophrenia is a serious and chronic mental health condition that can cause a range of symptoms, including hallucinations, delusions, disorganized speech and behavior, and social withdrawal. Individuals with schizophrenia may also experience cognitive impairment, such as difficulties with memory, attention, and problem-solving. It is important to note that schizophrenia is a complex disorder that can vary in presentation and severity among individuals.

Attention-deficit/hyperactivity disorder (ADHD) is a common neurodevelopmental disorder that affects both children and adults. Symptoms of ADHD may include inattention, hyperactivity, and impulsivity, which can impact various aspects of daily functioning, such as school performance, work productivity, and social relationships. It is important for individuals with ADHD to receive proper assessment and treatment in order to manage their symptoms and improve their quality of life.

Autism spectrum disorder (ASD) is a developmental disorder that affects communication, social interaction, and behavior. Individuals with ASD may have difficulties with verbal and nonverbal communication, social skills, and repetitive behaviors or interests. It is important for individuals with ASD to receive early intervention and support in order to develop their full potential and navigate the challenges associated with the condition.

Eating disorders are serious and potentially life-threatening conditions that can affect individuals of all ages and genders. Anorexia nervosa involves restrictive eating behaviors, body image disturbances, and an intense fear of gaining weight, while bulimia nervosa is characterized by binge eating followed by purging behaviors, such as vomiting or excessive exercise. Other types of eating disorders may involve excessive preoccupation with food, weight, and body image, as well as disordered eating patterns.

Substance use disorders involve the misuse or dependence on drugs or alcohol, which can lead to a range of physical, psychological, and social consequences. Symptoms of substance use disorders may include cravings, tolerance, withdrawal symptoms, and continued use despite negative consequences. It is important for individuals with substance use disorders to receive proper assessment and treatment in order to overcome their addiction and improve their overall well-being. By increasing awareness and knowledge of mental health and neurodevelopmental disorders, we can help reduce stigma, promote early intervention, and improve outcomes for those affected by these conditions. It is important for individuals to seek help from qualified professionals, such as psychologists, psychiatrists, and medical doctors, in order to receive proper assessment, diagnosis, and treatment for their symptoms. By working together as a community, we can support those in need and promote mental health and well-being for all.

- Seeking help and treatment options

Seeking help and treatment options for mental health concerns is an important step towards improving overall well-being and quality of life. It is essential to understand that seeking help is not a sign of weakness, but rather a sign of strength and self-awareness. There are various treatment options available for individuals struggling with mental health issues, ranging from therapy and counseling to medication and lifestyle changes. It is crucial to be informed about the different options available and to choose the approach that best suits your needs and preferences.

Therapy and counseling are common treatment options for individuals dealing with mental health issues. Therapy sessions with a trained professional can help individuals explore their thoughts and feelings, identify underlying issues, and develop coping strategies. Counseling can provide a safe and supportive space for individuals to talk about their concerns and receive guidance from a mental health professional. Different types of therapy, such as cognitive-behavioral therapy (CBT), dialectical behavior therapy (DBT), and psychodynamic therapy, may be recommended based on the individual's specific needs and goals for treatment.

Medication is another treatment option that may be used in conjunction with therapy or counseling for certain mental health conditions. Psychiatric medications, such as antidepressants, antianxiety medications, and mood stabilizers, can help alleviate symptoms and improve overall functioning. It is important to work closely with a psychiatrist or other mental health provider to determine the most appropriate medication and dosage for your specific condition. It is also important to closely monitor any potential side effects and make adjustments as needed.

In addition to therapy and medication, lifestyle changes can also play a significant role in managing mental health concerns. Engaging in regular exercise, maintaining a healthy diet, getting an adequate amount of sleep, and managing stress can all contribute to improved mental well-being. It is important to prioritize self-care and make time for activities that bring joy and fulfillment. Building a strong support network of friends, family, and other individuals who understand and validate your experiences can also be beneficial in promoting mental health.

When seeking help for mental health concerns, it is important to consider the various treatment options available and choose a approach that aligns with your values and goals. It is also important to seek help from qualified professionals who have experience and expertise in treating the specific mental health condition you are dealing with. Building a strong and collaborative relationship with your mental health provider can help ensure that you receive the best possible care and support.

It is important to remember that seeking help for mental health concerns is a courageous and proactive step towards improving your overall well-being. It is not something to be ashamed of or to be stigmatized. By reaching out for help and exploring treatment options, you are taking control of your mental health and working towards a healthier and happier future. Remember that you are not alone in your struggles and that there are resources and support available to help you on your journey towards healing and recovery.

Chapter 7: Technology and Social Media

- IMPACT OF TECHNOLOGY on adolescent behavior

Technology has become an integral part of everyday life for adolescents, shaping the way they communicate, learn, and socialize. With the rise of smartphones, social media, and instant messaging apps, adolescents are more connected to each other and the world around them than ever before. While technology has many benefits for adolescents, such as increased access to information and opportunities for communication, it also has a significant impact on their behavior.

One of the ways in which technology affects adolescent behavior is through the constant access to social media. Social media platforms like Instagram, Snapchat, and TikTok allow adolescents to connect with their peers, share photos and videos, and keep up with the latest trends. However, the pressure to maintain a perfect online persona can have negative effects on adolescent mental health. Studies have shown that excessive social media use can lead to feelings of loneliness, anxiety, and depression in adolescents. Additionally, the comparison of oneself to others on social media can contribute to low self-esteem and body image issues in adolescents.

Another way in which technology influences adolescent behavior is through the use of smartphones and mobile devices. Adolescents spend a significant amount of time on their phones, using them for everything from texting and browsing social media to playing games and watching videos. This constant exposure to screens can lead to a sedentary lifestyle and a lack of physical activity, which can have negative effects on adolescent health. In addition, the blue light emitted by screens can disrupt sleep patterns and lead to sleep deprivation in adolescents, which can impact their mood, cognitive function, and overall well-being.

Furthermore, technology has changed the way adolescents communicate with each other, often replacing face-to-face interactions with digital conversations. While technology has made it easier for adolescents to stay in touch with friends and family members, it can also lead to a decrease in the quality of their relationships. Some studies have found that excessive screen time can lead to a decrease in empathy and social skills in adolescents, as they may struggle to interpret nonverbal cues and emotions in person-to-person interactions. This can have long-term consequences for adolescent relationships, as well as their ability to form meaningful connections with others. While technology offers many benefits for adolescents, such as increased access to information and opportunities for communication, it also has potential drawbacks that must be considered. Parents, educators, and policymakers must work together to help adolescents navigate the digital world in a healthy and responsible way, promoting a balanced approach to technology use that supports their overall well-being. By understanding the impact of technology on adolescent behavior and taking steps to promote positive behaviors, we can help adolescents thrive in an increasingly digital world.

- Screen time and digital addiction

Screen time and digital addiction have become increasingly prevalent issues in today's society, with the widespread use of smartphones, tablets, computers, and other electronic devices. The term "screen time" refers to the amount of time a person spends using electronic devices with screens, such as watching TV, playing video games, or browsing the internet. While some screen time can be beneficial for educational and entertainment purposes, excessive screen time can have negative effects on individuals' physical and mental health. Digital addiction, also known as internet addiction or screen addiction, is a behavioral addiction characterized by a compulsive and excessive use of digital devices.

One of the main concerns surrounding screen time and digital addiction is the impact on individuals' mental health. Excessive screen time has been linked to feelings of loneliness, depression, anxiety, and stress. Spending too much time on electronic devices can lead to a sedentary lifestyle, which is associated with an increased risk of obesity, heart disease, and other health issues. In addition, the constant exposure to screens and digital content can overstimulate the brain and disrupt sleep patterns, leading to poor quality sleep and increased fatigue during the day.

Furthermore, digital addiction can have a negative impact on individuals' relationships and social interactions. People who are addicted to their digital devices may neglect their real-life relationships, such as family, friends, and colleagues, in favor of spending time online. This can lead to feelings of isolation and disconnection from others, as well as poor communication skills and difficulty in forming meaningful connections with others. In extreme cases, digital addiction can lead to social withdrawal and avoidance of real-world activities and responsibilities.

There are several signs and symptoms that may indicate a problem with screen time and digital addiction. These include a preoccupation with digital devices, an inability to control or limit screen time, neglect of real-life responsibilities and interests, withdrawal symptoms when not using digital devices, and using screens to cope with negative emotions or stress. If you or someone you know is exhibiting these signs and symptoms, it may be helpful to seek professional help and support to address the issue of digital addiction.

There are several strategies that can help individuals reduce their screen time and break free from digital addiction. One approach is to set limits on screen time and establish a daily routine that includes designated periods of device-free time. This can help individuals develop healthier habits and reduce the compulsive use of digital devices. In addition, engaging in physical activities, hobbies, and social interactions can help distract from the urge to use screens and provide alternative sources of enjoyment and fulfillment. It is important for individuals to be aware of the signs and symptoms of digital addiction and take steps to reduce their screen time and establish a healthy balance between digital and real-world activities. By setting limits on screen time, engaging in alternative activities, and seeking support when needed, individuals can break free from digital addiction and improve their quality of life.

- Balancing online and offline activities

In today's digital age, the balance between online and offline activities has become an increasingly important aspect of everyday life. With the rise of smartphones, social media, and online entertainment, it can be easy to get caught up in the virtual world and neglect our real-life relationships and responsibilities. Finding the right balance between online and offline activities is crucial for maintaining our mental and physical well-being, as well as fostering meaningful connections with others.

One of the key challenges in balancing online and offline activities is the constant presence of technology in our lives. From the moment we wake up to the moment we go to bed, we are bombarded with notifications, emails, and social media updates. It can be difficult to disconnect from our devices and carve out time for offline activities such as spending time with loved ones, exercising, or pursuing hobbies. This constant connectivity can lead to feelings of burnout, anxiety, and isolation if not managed properly.

To strike a healthy balance between online and offline activities, it is essential to set boundaries and establish a routine that prioritizes both aspects of our lives. This may involve setting designated times for checking emails and social media, turning off notifications during certain hours of the day, or setting aside specific days for unplugging entirely. By establishing clear boundaries, we can ensure that we are not allowing technology to dominate our lives and are making time for the things that truly matter to us.

In addition to setting boundaries, it is important to be mindful of how we are spending our time online and offline. Are we mindlessly scrolling through social media for hours on end, or are we engaging in activities that bring us joy and fulfillment? By being intentional about how we spend our time, we can ensure that we are not sacrificing meaningful relationships and experiences for the sake of technology. This may involve setting goals for ourselves, such as limiting screen time, scheduling regular outings with friends and family, or dedicating time each day for self-care activities.

Another important aspect of balancing online and offline activities is recognizing the impact that technology has on our mental health. Studies have shown that excessive screen time can lead to feelings of loneliness, depression, and anxiety. By being aware of how technology is affecting our well-being, we can make conscious choices to prioritize offline activities that promote our mental and emotional health. This may involve seeking out face-to-face interactions, spending time in nature, or engaging in activities that bring us joy and relaxation.

Ultimately, finding a balance between online and offline activities is a personal journey that requires self-awareness, intentionality, and mindfulness. By setting boundaries, being mindful of how we spend our time, and prioritizing activities that promote our well-being, we can create a harmonious relationship with technology and live a more fulfilling and balanced life. By finding this balance, we can enjoy the benefits of technology while also nurturing our relationships, pursuing our passions, and taking care of our mental and physical health.

Chapter 8: Academic and Career Development

- ACADEMIC PRESSURES and stress

Academic pressures and stress are common experiences for many students as they navigate the challenges of higher education. The demands of academic coursework, exams, deadlines, and expectations can create a significant amount of pressure for students, leading to feelings of stress, anxiety, and overwhelm. These pressures can stem from a variety of sources, including internal expectations, external pressures from family or peers, and societal norms around success and achievement.

One of the primary sources of academic pressure and stress for students is the rigorous demands of their coursework. The coursework in higher education is often challenging and time-consuming, requiring students to juggle multiple assignments, readings, projects, and exams simultaneously. The pressure to perform well academically can be exacerbated by the fast pace of academic deadlines and the high expectations placed on students by professors and institutions.

In addition to the academic demands of coursework, students may also feel pressure from external sources, such as family or peers. Family expectations around academic success can create added pressure for students, as they may feel a sense of obligation to excel in their studies in order to meet their family's expectations. Similarly, peer pressure to perform well academically can contribute to feelings of stress and anxiety, as students may compare themselves to their classmates and feel pressure to keep up with their academic achievements.

Societal norms around success and achievement can also play a significant role in contributing to academic pressure and stress for students. In many cultures, academic success is highly valued and seen as a key determinant of future success and happiness. This expectation can create pressure for students to excel academically in order to secure a promising future for themselves. The fear of failure or falling short of these expectations can create a significant amount of stress and anxiety for students as they navigate the challenges of higher education.

Managing academic pressures and stress is essential for students to maintain their well-being and succeed in their studies. There are a variety of strategies that students can use to cope with academic pressures and reduce feelings of stress and overwhelm. One effective strategy is to prioritize self-care and well-being by making time for activities that bring joy and relaxation, such as exercise, hobbies, or spending time with friends and family. Taking breaks and stepping away from the pressures of academia can help students recharge and refocus, making it easier to tackle academic challenges with a clear mind.

Another important strategy for managing academic pressures and stress is to seek support from professors, advisors, or counselors. These individuals can provide guidance, feedback, and resources to help students navigate the challenges of higher education and develop effective strategies for success. Seeking support from peers or joining study groups can also help students feel less isolated and more connected to a community of support. By implementing strategies to cope with academic pressures, prioritize self-care, and seek support from others, students can effectively manage stress and thrive in their academic pursuits. Taking care of one's well-being and seeking support when needed are essential components of navigating the challenges of higher education and achieving success.

- Career exploration and goal-setting

Career exploration and goal-setting are two critical components in the journey towards a successful and fulfilling professional life. In today's dynamic and ever-changing job market, it is essential for individuals to take the time to explore various career options and set clear and achievable goals. By doing so, individuals can ensure they are making informed decisions about their future and taking the necessary steps to reach their desired career destination.

One of the first steps in career exploration is to assess your interests, skills, values, and personality traits. This can be done through self-reflection, self-assessment tools, informational interviews, and job shadowing experiences. By gaining a clear understanding of what motivates you, what you excel at, and what you value in a work environment, you can start to identify potential career paths that align with who you are as a person. This self-awareness is essential in ensuring that you are pursuing a career that will bring you satisfaction and fulfillment in the long run.

Once you have identified potential career paths that align with your interests, skills, and values, it is important to conduct thorough research on the various industries and job roles within those fields. This can involve reading industry publications, attending networking events, and seeking out mentors who can provide valuable insights into the day-to-day realities of different professions. By gaining a deeper understanding of the opportunities and challenges within different industries, you can make more informed decisions about which career path is the best fit for you.

Setting clear and achievable career goals is also crucial in ensuring that you are on the right track towards your desired professional destination. Goals provide a roadmap for your career journey and help you stay focused and motivated as you work towards achieving them. When setting career goals, it is important to make them specific, measurable, achievable, relevant, and time-bound (SMART). This will help you track your progress, make adjustments as needed, and stay accountable to yourself.

In addition to setting long-term career goals, it is also beneficial to break them down into smaller, more manageable short-term goals. These short-term goals can help you make incremental progress towards your overall career objectives and provide you with a sense of accomplishment along the way. By celebrating small wins and milestones, you can stay motivated and inspired to continue working towards your larger career aspirations.

It is also important to remember that career exploration and goal-setting are ongoing processes that can evolve and change over time. As you gain more experience, knowledge, and insights into different industries and job roles, your career goals may shift and adapt to reflect your changing interests and priorities. It is important to remain flexible and open-minded as you navigate your career journey and be willing to make adjustments to your goals and plans as needed. By taking the time to assess your interests, skills, and values, conduct thorough research on various industries and job roles, and set clear and achievable career goals, you can ensure that you are on the right path towards building a career that aligns with who you are as a person. Remember that career exploration and goal-setting are ongoing processes that require self-reflection, research, flexibility, and perseverance. By investing time and effort into these areas, you can set yourself up for success in your chosen career path.

- Balancing academics with extracurricular activities

Balancing academics with extracurricular activities is a challenge that many students face during their time in school. While it can be difficult to juggle the demands of both academic work and extracurricular commitments, finding a balance between the two is essential for personal growth and success. In this essay, we will explore the benefits of participating in extracurricular activities, as well as strategies for effectively balancing these activities with academic responsibilities.

First and foremost, it is important to understand the value of participating in extracurricular activities. These activities offer students the opportunity to explore their interests, develop new skills, and build strong relationships with their peers. Whether it is joining a sports team, participating in a club or organization, or volunteering in the community, extracurricular activities can provide students with valuable experiences that enhance their overall education. In addition, involvement in extracurricular activities can also help students stand out to college admissions officers and potential employers, as it demonstrates a well-roundedness and a commitment to personal growth.

However, while extracurricular activities can offer numerous benefits, it is crucial for students to find a balance between these activities and their academic responsibilities. Without proper time management and prioritization, students run the risk of becoming overwhelmed and burning out. One strategy for achieving this balance is to create a schedule that allocates time for both academic work and extracurricular activities. By setting aside specific times each day for studying, attending classes, and participating in extracurricular activities, students can ensure that they are devoting adequate time and energy to both aspects of their lives.

Additionally, it is important for students to prioritize their commitments and learn to say no when necessary. While it can be tempting to take on multiple extracurricular activities in an effort to impress others, spreading oneself too thin can ultimately be detrimental to both academic performance and personal well-being. By carefully selecting which activities to participate in and being realistic about the time and energy required for each, students can avoid overextending themselves and ensure that they are able to maintain a healthy balance between academics and extracurricular activities.

Furthermore, communication is key when balancing academics with extracurricular activities. Students should inform their teachers, coaches, and club advisors about their commitments and work together to create a plan that allows for flexibility and support. By being open and honest about their schedule and any challenges they may be facing, students can receive the necessary guidance and assistance to succeed both academically and in their extracurricular pursuits. Additionally, seeking out mentors and role models who have successfully navigated the balance between academics and extracurricular activities can provide valuable insight and advice for students seeking to do the same. By recognizing the value of participating in extracurricular activities, creating a schedule that prioritizes both academic work and extracurricular commitments, learning to say no when necessary, and communicating effectively with teachers and advisors, students can achieve a healthy balance that allows them to excel in all areas of their lives. By approaching this challenge with a proactive and strategic mindset, students can cultivate valuable skills, experiences, and relationships that will benefit them both in school and beyond.

Chapter 9: Family Dynamics

- CHANGES IN FAMILY relationships during adolescence

During adolescence, individuals experience significant changes in their family relationships that can have a lasting impact on their overall development. This period of transition from childhood to adulthood is marked by physical, emotional, and social transformations, leading to shifts in the dynamics within the family unit. As adolescents strive for independence and autonomy, they may experience conflict with their parents and siblings as they navigate this challenging developmental stage.

One of the key changes that occurs in family relationships during adolescence is a shift in power dynamics. Adolescents often seek more autonomy and freedom to make their own decisions, which can create tension between them and their parents. This struggle for independence is a normal part of the developmental process as adolescents begin to develop their own identity separate from their family. Parents may struggle to balance their desire to protect their children with their need to allow them to make their own choices, leading to conflicts and power struggles within the family.

In addition to changes in power dynamics, adolescents may also experience changes in their emotional relationships with their family members. As they navigate the challenges of adolescence, they may become more emotionally distant from their parents, seeking support and validation from their peers instead. This shift in emotional bonds can be difficult for parents to navigate, as they may feel rejected or hurt by their child's increasing independence. However, it is important for parents to understand that this emotional distancing is a normal part of the adolescent development process and does not necessarily indicate a lack of love or respect for their family.

Furthermore, changes in family relationships during adolescence include shifts in communication patterns. As adolescents begin to assert their independence, they may become less willing to share their thoughts and feelings with their parents. This can lead to misunderstandings and conflicts within the family, as parents may feel shut out or disconnected from their child's life. It is important for parents to establish open lines of communication with their adolescents, creating a safe and supportive environment for them to express themselves without fear of judgment or criticism. By fostering open and honest communication, parents can strengthen their bond with their adolescent and navigate the challenges of this transitional period more effectively.

Another important aspect of changes in family relationships during adolescence is the impact on sibling relationships. As adolescents begin to assert their independence and develop their own identity, they may experience shifts in their relationships with their siblings. Sibling rivalry and competition may increase as adolescents vie for attention and resources within the family unit. However, sibling relationships can also be a source of support and understanding during this challenging time, as siblings often share similar experiences and can provide empathy and perspective to one another. It is important for parents to encourage positive sibling relationships and foster a sense of teamwork and cooperation within the family to navigate the challenges of adolescence effectively. Adolescents may experience shifts in power dynamics, emotional bonds, communication patterns, and sibling relationships as they navigate the challenges of this developmental stage. It is important for parents to understand and support their adolescents as they strive for independence and autonomy, fostering open communication and positive sibling relationships to navigate these changes effectively. By recognizing the unique needs and challenges of adolescents, parents can strengthen their bond with their children and support their overall development during this critical period of transition.

- Parenting styles and strategies

Parenting styles and strategies play a crucial role in shaping the development and well-being of children. Different parenting styles have been identified and studied by researchers to understand their impact on children's behavior, emotions, and overall adjustment. The four main parenting styles are authoritarian, authoritative, permissive, and uninvolved. Each style is characterized by different levels of demandingness and responsiveness.

The authoritarian parenting style is characterized by high levels of demandingness and low levels of responsiveness. Parents who adopt this style tend to be strict, controlling, and expect obedience from their children without offering much emotional support or warmth. This style can lead to children becoming obedient but may struggle with low self-esteem, social skills, and independence. Authoritarian parents often rely on punishment and discipline as their primary means of managing behavior.

In contrast, the authoritative parenting style is characterized by high levels of demandingness and responsiveness. Parents who use this style set clear expectations for their children but also provide warmth, support, and open communication. They are responsive to their children's needs and feelings while also setting limits and boundaries. This style has been found to be highly effective in promoting children's social, emotional, and academic development. Children raised by authoritative parents tend to be self-reliant, confident, and have high levels of self-esteem.

The permissive parenting style is characterized by low levels of demandingness and high levels of responsiveness. Parents who employ this style are indulgent, lenient, and avoid setting rules or boundaries for their children. They tend to be warm, nurturing, and overly lenient, often giving in to their children's demands and avoiding conflict. While permissive parents may have close relationships with their children, this style can lead to children lacking self-discipline, self-control, and respect for authority. Children raised in permissive households may struggle with academic performance, behavior problems, and lack of motivation.

Lastly, the uninvolved parenting style is characterized by low levels of demandingness and responsiveness. Parents who exhibit this style are often detached, neglectful, and emotionally disengaged from their children. They may provide for their children's basic needs but lack emotional support, supervision, and involvement in their children's lives. This style can have detrimental effects on children's development, leading to poor academic performance, social difficulties, and emotional problems. Children raised by uninvolved parents may struggle with low self-esteem, lack of independence, and have difficulty forming healthy relationships.

In addition to understanding different parenting styles, it is important to consider various parenting strategies that can enhance positive parenting practices and promote healthy child development. Some effective parenting strategies include setting clear and consistent rules and expectations, practicing positive discipline techniques, promoting open communication and active listening, fostering a warm and supportive relationship with your child, and modeling positive behavior and values. By implementing these strategies, parents can create a nurturing and supportive environment that fosters the social, emotional, and cognitive development of their children.

It is important to recognize that there is no one-size-fits-all approach to parenting, and each family may need to adapt their parenting style and strategies to meet the unique needs and characteristics of their children. It is also essential for parents to seek support, guidance, and resources to enhance their parenting skills and create a positive and healthy upbringing for their children. By understanding different parenting styles and strategies, parents can make informed decisions that promote their children's well-being and overall development.

- Sibling relationships and dynamics

These relationships are significant due to the amount of time spent together in childhood and adolescence, the emotional bonds that are formed, and the potential for lifelong support and companionship. Sibling dynamics can vary greatly depending on factors such as birth order, age gap, gender, personality differences, and life experiences. Understanding the complexities of sibling relationships can provide valuable insights into family dynamics, individual development, and social interactions.

Sibling Birth Order

One of the most influential factors in shaping sibling relationships is birth order. Birth order refers to the position a child occupies in the family hierarchy in relation to their siblings. For example, a first-born child is typically the oldest in the family, while a middle child is sandwiched between older and younger siblings. Birth order can play a role in shaping personality traits, behavior patterns, and relationship dynamics within the family. First-born children are often seen as responsible, conscientious, and ambitious, while later-born children may be more rebellious, creative, and outgoing. These differences in temperament can lead to various dynamics within sibling relationships, such as competition, cooperation, and mentorship.

Age Gap and Gender Differences

Another important factor in sibling relationships is the age gap between siblings and gender differences. The age gap between siblings can influence how they interact with each other, as well as the level of closeness and rivalry that exists between them. Siblings who are close in age may have more in common and engage in similar activities, while siblings who are farther apart in age may have different interests and experiences. Gender differences can also impact sibling relationships, as brothers and sisters may have different socialization experiences and expectations placed upon them. For example, girls may be socialized to be nurturing and empathetic, while boys may be encouraged to be competitive and assertive. These differences in socialization can create unique dynamics within sibling relationships based on gender roles and expectations.

Personality and Communication Styles

Personality differences can significantly influence sibling relationships and dynamics. Each sibling brings their own unique set of traits, behaviors, and communication styles to the relationship, which can either enhance or complicate their interactions. For example, one sibling may be introverted and prefer solitude, while another sibling may be extroverted and seek social connections. These differences in personality can lead to conflicts, misunderstandings, and challenges in communication. Siblings who have similar personalities and interests may have more harmonious relationships, while siblings who are very different may struggle to find common ground. Effective communication is essential for fostering healthy sibling relationships, as it helps siblings understand each other's perspectives, address conflicts, and strengthen their bond.

Sibling Rivalry and Conflict

Sibling rivalry is a common phenomenon that occurs in many sibling relationships. Sibling rivalry refers to the competition, jealousy, and conflict that can arise between siblings as they vie for attention, affection, and resources within the family. Rivalry can manifest in various forms, such as physical aggression, verbal arguments, emotional manipulation, and passive-aggressive behaviors. Sibling rivalry is often fueled by feelings of insecurity, inadequacy, and resentment, as siblings may perceive each other as threats to their own sense of self-worth and identity. Conflict resolution skills are essential for managing sibling rivalry and creating a more cooperative and supportive family environment. Siblings who learn to communicate effectively, express their emotions constructively, and resolve conflicts peacefully can strengthen their bond and build a more positive relationship.

Sibling Support and Connection

Despite the challenges and conflicts that can arise in sibling relationships, siblings also have the potential to provide each other with valuable support, understanding, and companionship. Siblings who share a strong bond and connection can be important sources of emotional, practical, and social support throughout their lives. They may offer each other guidance, encouragement, and empathy during times of need, as well as celebrate each other's achievements and milestones. Siblings can also serve as confidants, mentors, and role models for each other, offering different perspectives and insights that contribute to personal growth and development. Building a supportive and nurturing sibling relationship requires trust, respect, and mutual understanding, as well as a willingness to communicate openly and resolve conflicts peacefully.

SIBLING RELATIONSHIPS are complex and multifaceted, shaped by a variety of factors such as birth order, age gap, gender differences, personality traits, and communication styles. Understanding these dynamics can provide valuable insights into how siblings interact with each other, navigate conflicts, and build strong and lasting bonds. Sibling relationships have the potential to be sources of love, support, and companionship throughout one's life, fostering personal growth, emotional well-being, and social connections. By recognizing the unique dynamics of sibling relationships and cultivating positive communication skills, siblings can enhance their relationship, foster mutual understanding, and create a more harmonious and fulfilling family environment.

Chapter 10: Substance Use and Abuse

- RISK FACTORS FOR SUBSTANCE abuse in teenagers

Substance abuse among teenagers is a growing concern in today's society, with an increasing number of young individuals falling victim to the pitfalls of drug and alcohol addiction. There are a multitude of risk factors that can contribute to this troubling trend, ranging from genetic predispositions to environmental influences. By identifying and understanding these risk factors, we can work towards developing effective prevention and intervention strategies to help curb the tide of substance abuse among adolescents.

One of the most significant risk factors for substance abuse in teenagers is genetic predisposition. Numerous studies have shown a strong correlation between family history of addiction and an increased likelihood of developing substance abuse issues. Adolescents with a family history of substance abuse are at a higher risk of succumbing to the same addictive tendencies, due to a combination of genetic and environmental factors. Genetic predispositions can manifest in various ways, impacting an individual's susceptibility to addiction and their ability to resist the allure of drugs and alcohol. By recognizing these genetic risk factors, parents, educators, and healthcare professionals can take proactive measures to address and mitigate the potential for substance abuse in teenagers.

In addition to genetic predisposition, environmental influences also play a crucial role in shaping a teenager's risk of developing substance abuse issues. Adolescents who grow up in environments characterized by instability, trauma, or dysfunctional family dynamics are at an increased risk of turning to drugs and alcohol as a coping mechanism. Exposure to substance abuse within the family or peer group, lack of parental supervision, and poor academic performance are all environmental factors that can contribute to a teenager's susceptibility to substance abuse. Furthermore, societal factors such as easy access to drugs and alcohol, cultural attitudes towards substance use, and media influences can also play a significant role in shaping a teenager's attitudes and behaviors related to substance abuse. By addressing these environmental influences and creating supportive and nurturing environments for teenagers, we can help reduce the likelihood of substance abuse and provide the necessary resources and support to help adolescents make healthy and informed choices.

Another important risk factor for substance abuse in teenagers is psychological factors, such as mental health disorders and emotional distress. Adolescents who struggle with conditions such as depression, anxiety, trauma, or ADHD are more vulnerable to using drugs and alcohol as a means of self-medication or escapism. Substance abuse can provide temporary relief from emotional pain or alleviate symptoms of mental health disorders, leading to a dangerous cycle of dependency and addiction. It is crucial for parents, educators, and healthcare professionals to screen for and address underlying psychological issues in teenagers to prevent them from turning to substances as a coping mechanism. By providing appropriate mental health support and resources, we can help teenagers navigate their emotional struggles in a healthier and more productive manner, reducing the risk of substance abuse in the process.

Furthermore, peer influences and social relationships play a significant role in shaping a teenager's risk of developing substance abuse issues. Adolescents who have friends or peers who engage in drug and alcohol use are more likely to experiment with substances themselves, due to peer pressure, social norms, or a desire to fit in. Social dynamics within peer groups can exert a powerful influence on teenagers' behaviors and attitudes towards substance abuse, making it crucial for parents, educators, and community leaders to foster positive and healthy social relationships for adolescents. By promoting peer support and encouraging open communication about the risks and consequences of substance abuse, we can empower teenagers to make informed and responsible choices when it comes to drugs and alcohol.

It is important to recognize that substance abuse among teenagers is a complex and multifaceted issue that requires a comprehensive and multi-dimensional approach to prevention and intervention. By understanding the various risk factors that can contribute to substance abuse in adolescents, we can work towards developing targeted strategies to address each factor and reduce the overall prevalence of drug and alcohol addiction among young individuals. Through a combination of genetic, environmental, psychological, and social interventions, we can create a supportive and empowering environment for teenagers to thrive and make healthy choices, free from the grip of substance abuse. By working together as a community to address the root causes of substance abuse and provide the necessary support and resources for teenagers in need, we can help build a brighter and healthier future for the next generation.

- Preventive measures and interventions

Preventive measures and interventions play a crucial role in maintaining the health and well-being of individuals and populations. These strategies are designed to identify and address potential health risks before they escalate into more serious conditions. By implementing proactive measures, healthcare providers can reduce the overall burden of disease, improve quality of life, and minimize healthcare costs. In this discussion, we will explore the importance of preventive measures and interventions, examine different approaches to prevention, and identify key strategies for promoting healthy behaviors and reducing health risks.

Preventive measures encompass a wide range of interventions that are aimed at preventing the onset of diseases or conditions. These measures can include regular screenings, vaccinations, lifestyle modifications, and environmental changes. By identifying risk factors early on, healthcare providers can intervene before a disease progresses and becomes more difficult to treat. For example, screening programs for breast cancer can help detect tumors at an early stage when they are most treatable. Similarly, vaccinations can prevent the spread of infectious diseases such as measles, mumps, and flu, reducing the incidence of illness in communities.

There are three levels of prevention: primary, secondary, and tertiary. Primary prevention focuses on preventing the occurrence of a disease or condition before it develops. This can involve education and awareness campaigns, vaccination programs, and lifestyle modifications. Secondary prevention aims to detect and treat diseases in their early stages, preventing further complications and progression. This includes regular screenings, diagnostic tests, and early intervention programs. Tertiary prevention focuses on managing and treating existing conditions to prevent further complications and improve quality of life. This can involve rehabilitation programs, chronic disease management, and palliative care services.

Promoting healthy behaviors is a key component of preventive measures and interventions. Educating individuals about the importance of maintaining a healthy lifestyle can help prevent the onset of chronic diseases such as heart disease, diabetes, and obesity. Encouraging regular exercise, healthy eating habits, and stress management techniques can all contribute to a healthier lifestyle. Healthcare providers can also work with communities to create environments that support healthy choices, such as implementing smoke-free policies, promoting safe walking and biking paths, and increasing access to fresh fruits and vegetables.

In addition to lifestyle modifications, preventive measures also include regular health screenings and vaccinations. These interventions are designed to identify potential health risks early on and intervene before a disease progresses. For example, screenings for high blood pressure, cholesterol, and blood sugar levels can help identify individuals at risk for heart disease and diabetes. Vaccination programs can prevent the spread of infectious diseases and protect populations from outbreaks. By implementing these preventive measures, healthcare providers can significantly reduce the burden of disease and improve overall health outcomes.

Environmental changes can also play a role in preventing disease and promoting health. By creating safe and supportive environments, communities can reduce exposure to harmful substances and promote healthy behaviors. For example, implementing clean air regulations can reduce the incidence of respiratory diseases such as asthma and lung cancer. Improving access to clean water and sanitation facilities can prevent the spread of infectious diseases such as cholera and dysentery. By addressing environmental factors that contribute to poor health, communities can create conditions that support health and well-being. By focusing on prevention rather than just treatment, healthcare providers can reduce the burden of disease, improve quality of life, and minimize healthcare costs. Implementing proactive measures such as regular screenings, vaccinations, lifestyle modifications, and environmental changes can help identify and address potential health risks before they escalate into more serious conditions. By promoting healthy behaviors and creating supportive environments, communities can work together to prevent disease and promote health for all.

- **Resources for addiction treatment and recovery**

Addiction is a complex and chronic disease that affects millions of individuals worldwide, leading to devastating consequences for both the individuals struggling with the addiction and their loved ones. It is crucial to understand that addiction is not a moral failing or a lack of willpower, but rather a medical condition that requires comprehensive treatment and ongoing support for long-term recovery. Fortunately, there are a wide range of resources available for those seeking help with addiction treatment and recovery.

One of the first steps in the journey to recovery is seeking professional help from a qualified healthcare provider, such as a doctor or therapist. These healthcare professionals can assess the individual's specific needs and recommend a personalized treatment plan that may include a combination of therapy, medication, and support groups. Therapy, such as cognitive-behavioral therapy (CBT) or motivational interviewing, can help individuals explore the underlying causes of their addiction, develop coping mechanisms, and learn healthier ways to manage stress and emotions. Medication, such as buprenorphine for opioid addiction or naltrexone for alcohol addiction, can help reduce cravings and withdrawal symptoms, making it easier for individuals to focus on their recovery.

Support groups, such as Alcoholics Anonymous (AA) or Narcotics Anonymous (NA), can provide invaluable peer support and mentorship for individuals in recovery. These groups offer a safe and non-judgmental space for individuals to share their experiences, learn from others, and build a strong network of support. They promote the principles of honesty, accountability, and responsibility, which are essential for long-term sobriety. In addition to traditional support groups, there are also online forums and virtual meetings available for those who prefer to connect with others from the comfort of their own home.

In addition to therapy, medication, and support groups, there are also a variety of holistic approaches that can complement traditional addiction treatment. These may include mindfulness meditation, yoga, art therapy, and acupuncture, among others. These alternative therapies can help individuals reduce stress, improve their mental and emotional well-being, and find new ways to express themselves and cope with their addiction. It is important for individuals to explore and experiment with different modalities to find what works best for them and supports their recovery journey.

For individuals seeking 24/7 support and structure during early recovery, inpatient or residential treatment programs may be a good option. These programs offer a safe and structured environment where individuals can focus on their recovery without distractions or triggers from the outside world. Inpatient programs typically include individual and group therapy, educational sessions, recreational activities, and 24/7 medical and emotional support. Residential treatment programs may last anywhere from 30 days to several months, depending on the individual's needs and progress in treatment. These programs provide a strong foundation for individuals to build their recovery skills and develop a relapse prevention plan for when they transition back to their everyday lives.

After completing an inpatient or residential treatment program, many individuals benefit from transitioning to outpatient treatment and aftercare programs. Outpatient treatment allows individuals to continue to receive therapy, medication management, and support groups while living at home and maintaining their daily responsibilities. Aftercare programs, such as sober living homes or intensive outpatient programs (IOP), offer ongoing support and accountability for individuals as they navigate the challenges of transitioning back to their everyday lives. These programs can help individuals stay connected to their recovery community, build healthy habits and routines, and prevent relapse.

It is important for individuals in recovery to prioritize self-care and wellness as they work towards long-term sobriety. This may include regular exercise, adequate sleep, healthy eating, and mindfulness practices. By taking care of their physical, emotional, and spiritual well-being, individuals can reduce stress, improve their mood, and build resilience in the face of challenges. It is also important for individuals to cultivate strong social support networks and healthy relationships that reinforce their commitment to recovery and provide a sense of belonging and connection. From professional healthcare providers to support groups, holistic therapies, inpatient programs, outpatient treatment, and aftercare programs, there are many options for individuals to choose from based on their unique needs and preferences. It is important for individuals in recovery to explore and utilize these resources to develop a comprehensive and personalized approach to their healing journey. With dedication, commitment, and support, it is possible for individuals to overcome addiction and build a fulfilling and sober life.

Chapter 11: Sexual Health and Relationships

- PUBERTY AND SEXUAL development

Puberty is a period of rapid physical and psychological growth and development that occurs in adolescents, typically between the ages of 10 and 14 in girls and 12 and 16 in boys. This critical stage in human development is characterized by a cascade of hormonal changes that trigger the development of secondary sexual characteristics such as breast development in girls, facial hair growth in boys, and changes in body shape. These changes are driven by the release of hormones such as estrogen and testosterone, which play a crucial role in the maturation of the reproductive organs and the onset of sexual maturity.

Sexual development during puberty is a complex and multifaceted process that involves the interplay of biological, psychological, and social factors. In addition to the physical changes that occur during puberty, adolescents also experience a range of emotional and psychological changes as they navigate the transition from childhood to adulthood. This period of rapid growth and development can be challenging for many young people as they grapple with issues such as body image, self-esteem, and identity formation.

One of the key milestones of sexual development during puberty is the onset of menarche in girls and spermarche in boys, which marks the beginning of sexual maturity and the ability to reproduce. Menarche typically occurs around the age of 12 in girls and is characterized by the first menstrual period, while spermarche usually occurs around the age of 14 in boys and is marked by the production of sperm in the testes. These biological markers of sexual maturity are important milestones in the transition from childhood to adulthood and signal the beginning of the reproductive phase of life.

In addition to the physical changes that occur during puberty, adolescents also experience a range of psychological and emotional changes as they navigate the complexities of sexual development. This period of rapid growth and change can be challenging for many young people as they grapple with issues such as body image, self-esteem, and identity formation. Adolescents may also experience heightened emotions, mood swings, and increased sexual desire as they navigate the complexities of sexual development.

During puberty, adolescents also begin to develop their sexual identity, which refers to the way in which individuals view themselves as sexual beings and relate to others in a sexual manner. This process of identity formation is influenced by a range of factors, including biological factors such as genetics and hormones, as well as psychological and social factors such as family dynamics, peer relationships, and cultural norms. Adolescents may explore their sexual identity through experimentation with gender roles, sexual orientation, and intimate relationships as they seek to understand and define their own unique sense of self.

One of the key challenges of sexual development during puberty is the need for accurate and comprehensive information about sexual health and relationships. Adolescents may have many questions and concerns about their changing bodies and emerging sexual desires, and it is important for parents, teachers, and healthcare providers to provide guidance and support during this critical period of growth and development. Open and honest communication about sexual health, consent, and healthy relationships is essential for promoting positive sexual development and empowering young people to make informed choices about their sexual health and well-being. Sexual development during puberty is a critical aspect of this process, as adolescents navigate the physical, emotional, and psychological changes that accompany the onset of sexual maturity. By providing accurate information, guidance, and support, adults can help young people navigate the challenges of sexual development and empower them to make healthy and informed choices about their sexual health and well-being.

- Consent and healthy relationships

Consent is a fundamental and essential aspect of all healthy relationships, whether they be romantic, familial, or platonic. It is the cornerstone upon which trust, respect, and communication are built. In a romantic context, consent refers to both parties freely agreeing to engage in any form of physical intimacy or sexual activity. It is not only crucial for ensuring both individuals are comfortable and safe, but also for fostering a positive and mutually satisfying relationship. Consent must be explicit, ongoing, and enthusiastic, meaning that it is freely given without any form of coercion or pressure, and can be withdrawn at any time. Without consent, any form of physical contact can be considered a violation of personal boundaries and rights.

In order to establish a culture of consent within relationships, it is important for individuals to engage in open and honest communication with their partners. This involves discussing personal boundaries, desires, and preferences, as well as respecting the boundaries set by the other person. By creating a safe and non-judgmental space for dialogue, both parties can ensure that their needs and boundaries are being met, thus promoting a healthy and fulfilling relationship. It is also important to recognize that consent is not just about sexual activity, but also about respecting each other's autonomy and agency in all aspects of the relationship.

Furthermore, consent is not a one-time agreement, but an ongoing process that requires continuous communication and mutual understanding. It is important for individuals to check in with their partners regularly and to be responsive to any changes in their boundaries or comfort levels. By being attuned to each other's needs and feelings, both parties can ensure that their relationship remains respectful and consensual. Consent is a dynamic and fluid concept that may look different in various contexts and situations, which is why it is crucial for individuals to stay informed and educated on the topic.

In addition to communication and ongoing consent, it is important for individuals to be aware of power dynamics within relationships and how they can impact consent. Power imbalances, whether due to age, gender, social status, or other factors, can influence the ability of individuals to freely give or withhold consent. It is important for individuals to be mindful of these dynamics and to actively work towards creating a relationship that is based on equality, respect, and mutual understanding. By acknowledging and addressing any potential power differentials, individuals can create a more equitable and consensual partnership. By establishing a culture of consent through open and honest communication, ongoing dialogue, and awareness of power dynamics, individuals can create a safe and respectful environment that promotes mutual understanding and fulfillment. It is important for individuals to be proactive in seeking consent and respecting each other's boundaries, as well as to remain informed and educated on the topic. Ultimately, consent is about recognizing and respecting each other's autonomy and agency, and ensuring that all interactions are based on mutual agreement and enthusiasm.

- Safe sex practices and contraception

Safe sex practices and contraception are essential components of sexual health and well-being. It is important for individuals to understand the importance of using protection during sexual activity to reduce the risk of sexually transmitted infections (STIs) and unintended pregnancies. Contraception, also known as birth control, refers to methods used to prevent pregnancy. There are a variety of contraceptive methods available, ranging from barrier methods like condoms and diaphragms to hormonal methods like birth control pills and intrauterine devices (IUDs).

One of the most commonly used methods of contraception is the condom, which is a barrier method that helps prevent the transmission of STIs and reduces the risk of pregnancy. Condoms are typically made of latex or polyurethane and are worn over the penis during sexual activity. It is important to use condoms correctly and consistently to ensure their effectiveness. When used consistently and correctly, condoms are highly effective at preventing the transmission of STIs, including HIV, gonorrhea, and chlamydia.

In addition to condoms, there are other types of barrier methods that can be used to prevent pregnancy and protect against STIs. For example, diaphragms are another type of barrier method that is inserted into the vagina before sexual activity to prevent sperm from reaching the cervix. Diaphragms are typically used in conjunction with spermicide to increase their effectiveness. Another barrier method is the cervical cap, which is a small, silicone cup that is inserted into the vagina before sexual activity. Like the diaphragm, the cervical cap is used with spermicide to prevent pregnancy.

Hormonal methods of contraception, such as birth control pills and IUDs, are also highly effective at preventing pregnancy. Birth control pills work by preventing ovulation, while IUDs work by either releasing hormones that prevent ovulation or by creating a physical barrier to sperm. Birth control pills must be taken daily to be effective, while IUDs are inserted into the uterus by a healthcare provider and can provide long-lasting protection against pregnancy. It is important for individuals to discuss their options with a healthcare provider to determine the best method of contraception for their needs and lifestyle.

In addition to using contraception, it is important for individuals to practice safe sex to reduce the risk of STIs. This includes using condoms and other barrier methods consistently and correctly, as well as getting tested for STIs regularly. It is also important to communicate openly and honestly with sexual partners about sexual history and STI status. By practicing safe sex and using contraception, individuals can protect their sexual health and well-being.

It is important for individuals to be informed about safe sex practices and contraception to make healthy and responsible choices about their sexual health. By using contraception consistently and correctly, individuals can prevent unintended pregnancies and protect against STIs. Additionally, practicing safe sex and communicating openly with sexual partners can help reduce the risk of STIs and promote sexual health. It is important for individuals to prioritize their sexual health and well-being by taking proactive steps to protect themselves and their partners.

Chapter 12: Gender and Sexuality

- UNDERSTANDING GENDER identity and sexual orientation

Gender identity and sexual orientation are complex and multifaceted aspects of an individual's identity. They are often mistakenly conflated, but in reality, they are distinct concepts that are separate yet interconnected. Gender identity refers to one's internal sense of their own gender, which may or may not align with the sex assigned to them at birth. Sexual orientation, on the other hand, refers to one's emotional, romantic, or sexual attraction to others. While these concepts are separate, they can certainly influence and interact with each other in a variety of ways.

Gender identity is not always binary; it exists on a spectrum that includes a wide range of identities beyond just male and female. Some individuals may identify as non-binary, genderqueer, or genderfluid, among other identities. It is important to respect and validate each person's self-identified gender identity, even if it does not conform to traditional societal norms. Gender identity is deeply personal and may evolve over time as individuals explore and better understand themselves.

Sexual orientation is also diverse and encompasses a wide range of identities, including but not limited to heterosexual, homosexual, bisexual, pansexual, and asexual. It is important to recognize that sexual orientation is not a choice but rather an inherent part of who a person is. Individuals should be free to express their sexual orientation without fear of discrimination or prejudice.

It is crucial to understand that gender identity and sexual orientation are separate from physical anatomy. Gender identity is about how one views themselves within their own mind, while sexual orientation is about who one is attracted to emotionally, romantically, and sexually. It is not appropriate to assume someone's gender identity or sexual orientation based on their physical appearance or other external factors. Respect for diversity and individuality is essential in creating a supportive and inclusive environment for people of all gender identities and sexual orientations.

There is a growing awareness and acceptance of gender diversity and the LGBTQ+ community in society, but discrimination and stigma still exist. Transgender and gender non-conforming individuals, in particular, face discrimination and marginalization in many aspects of life, including healthcare, employment, and education. It is important to advocate for equal rights and protections for all individuals, regardless of their gender identity or sexual orientation.

Education and awareness are key in promoting understanding and acceptance of gender identity and sexual orientation. Organizations and institutions can provide training and resources to help individuals better understand these concepts and how they can support and affirm individuals of all gender identities and sexual orientations. By fostering a culture of respect, inclusivity, and diversity, we can create a more equitable and accepting society for all. Gender identity and sexual orientation are fundamental aspects of who we are as individuals, and everyone deserves to be treated with dignity and respect, regardless of how they identify or who they love.

- Support for LGBTQ+ teenagers

Support for LGBTQ+ teenagers is crucial for their overall well-being and development. Adolescence is already a challenging time for many young people as they navigate physical, emotional, and social changes. LGBTQ+ teenagers face unique challenges related to their sexual orientation and gender identity, including discrimination, rejection, and lack of acceptance from family, friends, and society at large. This can lead to feelings of isolation, depression, and anxiety. Therefore, it is essential for LGBTQ+ teenagers to have access to supportive resources and services that can help them navigate these challenges and thrive.

One of the key sources of support for LGBTQ+ teenagers is their family. Family acceptance and support can have a significant impact on the mental health and well-being of LGBTQ+ teenagers. Research has shown that LGBTQ+ teenagers who are supported by their families are less likely to experience depression, anxiety, and suicidal ideation. Family support can come in many forms, including open communication, acceptance of their sexual orientation and gender identity, and advocacy for their rights and well-being. It is important for parents and caregivers to educate themselves about LGBTQ+ issues and to create a safe and affirming environment for their LGBTQ+ teenager.

In addition to family support, LGBTQ+ teenagers can benefit from support from their schools and communities. School is a significant environment for teenagers, and it is essential for LGBTQ+ teenagers to feel safe, valued, and supported at school. Schools can create safe spaces, such as Gay-Straight Alliances (GSAs) or LGBTQ+ support groups, where LGBTQ+ teenagers can connect with peers who share similar experiences. Schools can also provide LGBTQ+ inclusive curriculum and policies that protect the rights of LGBTQ+ students. Community organizations and resources, such as LGBTQ+ youth centers, can also offer support and resources for LGBTQ+ teenagers.

Mental health support is another critical aspect of support for LGBTQ+ teenagers. LGBTQ+ teenagers are at a higher risk for mental health issues, such as depression, anxiety, and suicidal ideation, due to the discrimination and stigma they face. It is important for LGBTQ+ teenagers to have access to mental health services that are LGBTQ+ affirming and inclusive. Mental health professionals who are knowledgeable about LGBTQ+ issues can provide counseling and support specifically tailored to the needs of LGBTQ+ teenagers. It is also important for LGBTQ+ teenagers to have access to crisis intervention services, such as hotlines or online chat services, in case of emergencies.

It is essential for LGBTQ+ teenagers to have access to resources and support that affirm their identities and promote their well-being. LGBTQ+ teenagers are a diverse group with unique experiences and needs, and it is important for support services to be inclusive and affirming of this diversity. LGBTQ+ teenagers may identify as lesbian, gay, bisexual, transgender, queer, questioning, or another identity on the LGBTQ+ spectrum. It is important for support services to be inclusive of all identities within the LGBTQ+ community and to address the specific needs and challenges faced by each identity. LGBTQ+ teenagers face unique challenges related to their sexual orientation and gender identity, including discrimination, rejection, and lack of acceptance. It is essential for LGBTQ+ teenagers to have access to supportive resources and services that can help them navigate these challenges and thrive. Family support, school and community support, mental health support, and inclusive resources and services are all key aspects of support for LGBTQ+ teenagers. By providing affirming and inclusive support, we can help LGBTQ+ teenagers feel accepted, valued, and empowered to live authentic and fulfilling lives.

- Addressing discrimination and prejudice

Discrimination and prejudice are pervasive issues that continue to plague societies around the world. These harmful attitudes and behaviors stem from biases and stereotypes that individuals hold about certain groups of people based on factors such as race, ethnicity, gender, religion, sexual orientation, or disability. Discrimination occurs when these biases manifest in harmful actions or treatment towards individuals or groups, while prejudice refers to the negative attitudes and beliefs that fuel such discriminatory behavior. It is crucial for individuals, organizations, and institutions to address and challenge discrimination and prejudice in order to promote equality, fairness, and social justice.

One of the key ways to address discrimination and prejudice is through education and awareness. By increasing understanding and empathy among individuals, we can work to dismantle harmful stereotypes and biases that contribute to discrimination. Education can take many forms, from formal classroom instruction to informal discussions and workshops. It is important to engage in open and honest conversations about privilege, power dynamics, and systemic inequalities in order to confront the underlying causes of discrimination. By promoting a culture of learning and growth, we can create a more inclusive society where all individuals feel respected and valued.

Another important aspect of addressing discrimination and prejudice is through policy and legislation. Laws and regulations play a crucial role in safeguarding the rights of marginalized groups and holding perpetrators of discrimination accountable for their actions. It is essential for governments and institutions to implement and enforce anti-discrimination laws that protect individuals from discrimination based on their identity or characteristics. Additionally, policies that promote diversity and inclusion in the workplace, education system, and other settings can help create environments where discrimination and prejudice are not tolerated.

In addition to education and policy, it is also essential to promote empathy and understanding among individuals in order to combat discrimination and prejudice. Empathy allows us to connect with others on a human level and recognize the shared humanity that unites us all. By listening to the experiences and perspectives of those who have been marginalized or discriminated against, we can gain a deeper understanding of the impact of our words and actions. Building empathy requires us to step outside of our own perspectives and biases and truly listen to the stories and struggles of others. Through empathy, we can cultivate compassion and respect for all individuals, regardless of their background or identity.

Furthermore, fostering a culture of inclusion and belonging is crucial in addressing discrimination and prejudice. Inclusive environments celebrate diversity and create spaces where all individuals feel welcome and valued. It is important for organizations and institutions to actively work towards creating inclusive policies, practices, and spaces that accommodate the needs and experiences of all individuals. This can include initiatives such as diversity training, mentorship programs for underrepresented groups, and creating safe spaces for individuals to express their identities and experiences. By prioritizing inclusion and belonging, we can create a more equitable and just society for all individuals. By increasing awareness and understanding of the harmful impacts of discrimination, we can work towards dismantling biases and stereotypes that perpetuate prejudice. Through the implementation of anti-discrimination laws and policies, we can create environments that promote equality and protect the rights of marginalized groups. Empathy and compassion are essential in building connections and fostering understanding among individuals from different backgrounds. To draw to a close, by creating inclusive spaces that celebrate diversity and promote a sense of belonging, we can work towards creating a more equitable and just society for all individuals. It is up to each of us to take responsibility for challenging discrimination and prejudice in our communities and working towards a more inclusive and respectful world.

Chapter 13: Cultural and Ethical Considerations

- IMPACT OF CULTURE and values on adolescent behavior

Culture and values play a significant role in shaping the behavior of adolescents. Adolescence is a crucial period in an individual's life where they undergo enormous physical, emotional, and cognitive changes. During this time, teenagers are more susceptible to external influences, including those of their culture and values, which can greatly impact their behavior and decision-making.

Culture refers to the shared beliefs, customs, traditions, and practices of a particular group of people. It encompasses the way individuals think, feel, and act, and is deeply ingrained in their identity. Adolescents are heavily influenced by the culture in which they are raised, as they learn societal norms and values from their families, peers, and communities. For example, in collectivist cultures, such as many Asian societies, the emphasis is on group harmony and interdependence. This focus on community and relationships can influence adolescents to prioritize the needs of the group over their individual desires, leading to behaviors that promote social cohesion and cooperation.

Values are the core principles and beliefs that individuals hold dear and guide their behavior. These values are often instilled in adolescence through socialization processes and play a critical role in shaping their ethical and moral decision-making. For instance, if a teenager grows up in a family that places a high value on honesty and integrity, they are likely to exhibit behaviors that align with these principles, such as telling the truth and acting with integrity in their interactions with others. On the contrary, if they are raised in an environment where material wealth and success are prioritized, they may engage in behaviors that focus on achieving financial success at any cost.

The impact of culture and values on adolescent behavior can be seen in various aspects of their lives, including their academic performance, relationships, and mental health. Adolescents who come from cultures that prioritize education and knowledge tend to place a high value on academic achievement and may work diligently to excel in their studies. On the other hand, teenagers who are raised in cultures that do not emphasize education may be less motivated to succeed academically and may engage in behaviors that hinder their educational attainment.

In terms of relationships, cultural norms and values can greatly influence the way adolescents interact with others. For example, in cultures where respect for elders is highly valued, teenagers are more likely to demonstrate deference and obedience towards older family members and authority figures. In contrast, in cultures that promote individualism and self-expression, adolescents may prioritize their own needs and desires in their relationships, sometimes at the expense of others.

Furthermore, the impact of culture and values on adolescent behavior extends to their mental health and well-being. Adolescents who are raised in cultures that stigmatize mental health issues may be less likely to seek help for their emotional struggles and may resort to unhealthy coping mechanisms, such as substance abuse or self-harm. Conversely, teenagers who come from cultures that prioritize mental health and well-being may be more open to seeking support from mental health professionals and engaging in healthy coping strategies to manage their emotions.

It is essential for parents, educators, and policymakers to recognize the influence of culture and values on adolescent behavior and provide adolescents with the necessary support and resources to navigate these influences in a positive and healthy way. By fostering an environment that promotes cultural awareness and values-based decision-making, adults can help adolescents develop a strong sense of identity and a moral compass that guides them towards responsible and ethical behavior. Additionally, incorporating culturally sensitive practices and interventions in schools and communities can help create an inclusive and supportive environment that empowers adolescents to thrive and reach their full potential. Ultimately, by understanding and addressing the impact of culture and values on adolescent behavior, we can create a more compassionate and understanding society that values the diverse perspectives and experiences of young people.

- Addressing cultural stereotypes and biases

Cultural stereotypes and biases are pervasive in society, shaping our perceptions and interactions with people from different backgrounds. These stereotypes are often based on limited or inaccurate information and can lead to unfair treatment, discrimination, and prejudice. Addressing cultural stereotypes and biases is essential in creating a more inclusive and equitable society.

One way to address cultural stereotypes and biases is through education and awareness. By educating ourselves about different cultures and challenging our assumptions, we can begin to dismantle stereotypes and biases. This can involve learning about the history, traditions, and values of different cultures, as well as questioning the stereotypes we may hold about certain groups. Education can help us to see the complexity and diversity within cultural groups, rather than reducing them to simplistic stereotypes.

Another important step in addressing cultural stereotypes and biases is promoting diversity and inclusion in all aspects of society. This can involve creating spaces where people from different cultural backgrounds feel valued and respected, as well as actively seeking out diverse perspectives and voices. By promoting diversity and inclusion, we can challenge stereotypes and biases, and create a more welcoming and inclusive environment for all individuals.

It is also important to recognize our own biases and prejudices and work to overcome them. This can involve reflecting on our own beliefs and attitudes, as well as seeking feedback from others about how our words and actions may be influenced by stereotypes. By acknowledging and addressing our own biases, we can become more aware of how they impact our interactions with others and work to overcome them.

In addition to education and awareness, it is important to advocate for policies and practices that promote diversity and equality. This can involve supporting initiatives that promote diversity and inclusion in the workplace, schools, and other institutions, as well as advocating for fair and equal treatment for all individuals, regardless of their cultural background. By advocating for policies that address cultural stereotypes and biases, we can help to create a more just and equitable society for all individuals. By challenging our assumptions, promoting diversity and inclusion, recognizing our own biases, and advocating for change, we can work towards creating a more inclusive and equitable society that values the contributions of all individuals, regardless of their cultural background. By taking these steps, we can help to create a society where diversity is celebrated and differences are embraced, rather than used as a basis for discrimination and prejudice.

- Moral development and ethical decision-making

Moral development and ethical decision-making are key components of personal and professional growth. It is essential for individuals to have a solid understanding of ethical principles and moral values in order to navigate the complexities of life and make sound decisions in various situations. This topic has been of interest to philosophers, psychologists, and educators for centuries, as it plays a crucial role in shaping human behavior and shaping societies.

Moral development refers to the process through which individuals acquire moral values, beliefs, and behaviors. This process is influenced by a variety of factors, including genetics, upbringing, culture, and social environment. Psychologist Lawrence Kohlberg proposed a model of moral development, known as the Kohlberg's stages of moral development, which outlines the different stages through which individuals progress in their understanding of morality and ethical principles. According to Kohlberg, there are six stages of moral development, ranging from preconventional morality to postconventional morality. At each stage, individuals are faced with moral dilemmas that challenge their existing beliefs and values, prompting them to reconsider and develop more complex and nuanced moral reasoning.

Ethical decision-making, on the other hand, refers to the process through which individuals make choices that are consistent with ethical principles and values. Ethical decision-making is not always straightforward, as individuals are often faced with conflicting moral obligations and competing interests. In order to make ethical decisions, individuals must consider the consequences of their actions, the rights and interests of others, and the principles that guide ethical behavior. This requires a high level of moral reasoning and the ability to make judgments that are fair, just, and informed.

There are a number of factors that can influence moral development and ethical decision-making. For example, individuals who are exposed to positive role models and ethical principles from a young age are more likely to develop strong moral values and make ethical decisions. On the other hand, individuals who are exposed to unethical behavior or who lack moral guidance may struggle to develop a strong moral compass and may be more susceptible to making unethical choices. Additionally, cultural and societal factors can also play a significant role in shaping moral development and ethical decision-making. Different cultures have different moral values and ethical principles, and individuals may be influenced by the values and norms of their society.

Education also plays a critical role in fostering moral development and ethical decision-making. Schools and universities have a responsibility to teach students about moral values, ethical principles, and the importance of making ethical decisions. By incorporating ethics education into the curriculum, educators can help students develop a strong moral compass and the skills they need to make ethical decisions in their personal and professional lives. This includes teaching students about the importance of honesty, integrity, respect for others, and empathy, as well as providing them with opportunities to practice ethical decision-making in real-world scenarios. By understanding the principles of moral development and ethical decision-making, individuals can navigate the complexities of life and make sound choices that are consistent with their values and beliefs. Through education, positive role modeling, and exposure to diverse perspectives, individuals can develop a strong moral compass and the skills they need to make ethical decisions in a variety of situations. Ultimately, ethical decision-making is not just about following rules or adhering to codes of conduct, but about cultivating a deep sense of moral responsibility and integrity that guides one's actions and decisions.

Chapter 14: School and Community Engagement

- INVOLVEMENT IN SCHOOL and community activities

Being actively involved in school and community activities can have a profound impact on a student's overall development and well-being. By participating in extracurricular activities, students have the opportunity to cultivate important skills such as teamwork, leadership, time management, and communication. These skills are not only valuable in academic settings but also in preparing students for future success in their careers and personal lives.

In addition to developing crucial skills, involvement in school and community activities can also enhance a student's sense of belonging and connectedness. Engaging in extracurricular activities allows students to form meaningful relationships with their peers and mentors, creating a support system that can help them navigate the challenges of adolescence. This sense of belonging can boost a student's self-esteem and confidence, leading to increased motivation and academic performance.

Furthermore, participation in school and community activities can broaden a student's perspective and foster a sense of social responsibility. By engaging with diverse groups of peers and community members, students learn to appreciate different perspectives and cultures, promoting empathy and understanding. This exposure to new ideas and experiences can spark an interest in social issues and inspire students to become active citizens who contribute positively to their communities.

Moreover, involvement in extracurricular activities can provide students with opportunities for personal growth and self-discovery. By trying out different hobbies and interests, students can uncover hidden talents and passions, leading to a greater sense of purpose and fulfillment. Exploring new activities can also help students build resilience and adaptability, as they learn to navigate challenges and setbacks in a supportive environment.

In today's fast-paced and competitive world, the benefits of involvement in school and community activities cannot be overstated. As students face increasing pressure to excel academically and stand out in college and job applications, participation in extracurricular activities can set them apart and demonstrate their well-roundedness. Colleges and employers often look for candidates who have demonstrated leadership, teamwork, and a commitment to their communities, qualities that are developed through engagement in extracurricular activities. By participating in extracurricular activities, students can develop important skills, foster meaningful relationships, expand their worldview, and discover their passions. This holistic approach to education not only enhances academic success but also promotes personal growth and social responsibility. Therefore, it is essential for students to actively engage in extracurricular activities to maximize their potential and become well-rounded individuals who are prepared to succeed in all aspects of life.

- Volunteer opportunities and leadership development

Volunteer opportunities provide invaluable experiences for individuals looking to enhance their leadership skills and make a positive impact on their communities. By volunteering, individuals have the chance to gain hands-on experience in a variety of roles and settings, while also developing key leadership competencies such as communication, teamwork, problem-solving, and decision-making. These experiences can be instrumental in shaping individuals into effective leaders who are capable of inspiring and motivating others towards a common goal.

One of the key benefits of volunteering is the opportunity to take on leadership roles and responsibilities within an organization or community project. This hands-on experience allows individuals to test their leadership abilities in a real-world setting, where they can learn from both their successes and failures. By leading a team of volunteers or managing a project, individuals can develop key skills such as delegation, conflict resolution, and time management, which are essential for effective leadership.

Furthermore, volunteering provides individuals with the chance to collaborate with others from diverse backgrounds and perspectives. This diversity of thought and experience can help individuals expand their understanding of different leadership styles and approaches, while also learning how to effectively communicate and work with a range of personality types. By working with others towards a common goal, individuals can develop their ability to build and maintain relationships, which is crucial for effective leadership in any setting.

In addition to developing key leadership skills, volunteering can also help individuals build a strong network of contacts within their community or industry. By connecting with other volunteers, organizational leaders, and community members, individuals can gain valuable insights and advice on how to further develop their leadership abilities. These connections can also provide individuals with future opportunities for leadership roles or professional development, as they build a reputation for their dedication and expertise in their chosen field.

Moreover, volunteering can help individuals build their confidence and self-esteem as they see the tangible impact of their efforts on their community. By taking on leadership roles and responsibilities, individuals can experience the satisfaction of making a positive difference in the lives of others, which can boost their sense of purpose and fulfillment. This sense of accomplishment can further motivate individuals to continue developing their leadership skills and seeking out new opportunities for growth and development. By taking on leadership roles within a volunteer organization or community project, individuals can gain hands-on experience, develop key competencies, and build a strong network of contacts. Through collaboration with others and the satisfaction of seeing the results of their efforts, individuals can enhance their confidence, self-esteem, and sense of purpose. In this way, volunteering can serve as a powerful catalyst for leadership development and personal growth.

- Advocacy for social causes and community issues

Advocacy for social causes and community issues is a crucial aspect of creating positive change in society. It involves individuals or groups working to raise awareness, promote policies, and create solutions for issues that affect communities. Advocates come from various backgrounds and often have personal experiences that drive their passion for a particular cause. They use their voices and platforms to push for change and fight for social justice.

One of the key roles of advocacy is to bring attention to issues that may be overlooked or ignored by the larger society. This can include issues such as poverty, discrimination, environmental degradation, and access to healthcare. By shining a light on these issues, advocates can help to educate the public and policymakers about the importance of addressing these problems and finding solutions. This awareness-building is essential in creating a sense of urgency and mobilizing support for change.

Advocacy can take many forms, from grassroots activism to lobbying policymakers and working within established organizations. Grassroots advocates often work on the ground in communities, organizing rallies, protests, and community events to raise awareness about an issue and mobilize support. They may also work to build relationships with local leaders and policymakers to push for policy changes that benefit their communities. Lobbyists, on the other hand, work within government institutions to advocate for specific policies or legislation that address social issues.

In addition to raising awareness and advocating for policy change, advocates also play a crucial role in providing support and resources to those affected by social issues. This can include offering direct services such as counseling, legal assistance, or healthcare, as well as connecting individuals with community resources and support networks. By offering this support, advocates can help individuals navigate the challenges they face and empower them to take action to improve their own lives and communities.

Advocacy for social causes and community issues is not without its challenges. Advocates often face resistance from those who are in positions of power or who benefit from the status quo. They may also face obstacles such as lack of funding, limited resources, and burnout from the emotional toll of the work. Despite these challenges, advocates persist in their efforts to create positive change and improve the lives of individuals and communities. Advocates work tirelessly to raise awareness, promote policy change, and provide support to those in need. Through their efforts, advocates play a vital role in addressing social issues and working towards positive change. It is important for individuals to support advocacy efforts and get involved in advocating for causes they care about. Together, we can create a better future for all members of society.

Chapter 15: Mindfulness and Self-care

- BENEFITS OF MINDFULNESS and self-care practices

Mindfulness and self-care practices have gained increasing popularity in recent years as individuals seek ways to improve their physical, mental, and emotional well-being. These practices involve being fully present and aware of one's thoughts, feelings, and surroundings, and taking deliberate actions to nurture one's overall health and happiness. The benefits of mindfulness and self-care practices are numerous, ranging from reduced stress and anxiety to improved focus and concentration. By incorporating these practices into our daily lives, we can enhance our quality of life and increase our resilience in the face of challenges.

One of the key benefits of mindfulness and self-care practices is their ability to reduce stress and anxiety. In today's fast-paced world, many of us are constantly juggling multiple responsibilities and facing high levels of pressure in both our personal and professional lives. This chronic stress can have a detrimental impact on our physical and mental health, leading to a range of issues such as insomnia, digestive problems, and mood swings. By engaging in mindfulness practices such as meditation, deep breathing exercises, and yoga, we can learn to calm our minds and bodies, reduce our stress levels, and cultivate a sense of inner peace and tranquility.

In addition to reducing stress, mindfulness and self-care practices can also help us manage anxiety and other mental health conditions. Anxiety disorders are among the most common mental health issues worldwide, affecting millions of individuals of all ages. Symptoms of anxiety can manifest in various ways, such as racing thoughts, restlessness, and panic attacks. By practicing mindfulness techniques like mindfulness meditation and body scans, we can learn to observe our anxious thoughts and feelings without judgment, and develop the skills to respond to them in a more constructive and compassionate way. This can lead to a significant reduction in anxiety symptoms and an increased sense of control over our mental well-being.

Furthermore, mindfulness and self-care practices have been shown to improve focus and concentration, which can enhance our productivity and performance in various aspects of our lives. In a world filled with distractions and information overload, it can be challenging to stay engaged and attentive to the task at hand. However, by training our minds to be more present and focused through practices like mindful breathing and mindful eating, we can sharpen our cognitive abilities and improve our ability to concentrate on the task at hand. This can lead to enhanced creativity, problem-solving skills, and overall cognitive function, enabling us to achieve our goals more efficiently and effectively.

Another important benefit of mindfulness and self-care practices is their ability to foster self-compassion and self-acceptance. In today's society, many of us struggle with feelings of inadequacy, self-doubt, and self-criticism, which can erode our self-esteem and confidence over time. By practicing self-care activities such as journaling, self-reflection, and self-care routines, we can cultivate a greater sense of self-awareness and self-compassion, and learn to treat ourselves with kindness and understanding. This can help us develop a more positive relationship with ourselves, build resilience in the face of challenges, and enhance our overall sense of well-being and fulfillment.

Furthermore, mindfulness and self-care practices can have a profound impact on our physical health and well-being. The mind-body connection is a powerful force, and our mental and emotional states can have a direct impact on our physical health. By engaging in practices like mindfulness meditation, gentle yoga, and mindful eating, we can reduce our risk of chronic diseases such as heart disease, diabetes, and obesity, and improve our overall physical fitness and vitality. Mindfulness practices can also help us develop healthier habits and behaviors, such as getting regular exercise, eating a balanced diet, and getting an adequate amount of sleep, all of which are essential for maintaining optimal physical health and well-being. By incorporating these practices into our daily lives, we can reduce stress and anxiety, improve focus and concentration, enhance self-compassion and self-acceptance, and promote overall health and vitality. Whether it is through mindfulness meditation, yoga, journaling, or other self-care activities, taking the time to nurture our minds, bodies, and spirits can lead to a profound transformation in our lives and enable us to live more fully and authentically. So, why not start today. Take a few moments to breathe deeply, center yourself, and connect with the present moment - your future self will thank you for it.

- Stress management techniques

Stress is an inevitable part of life that affects everyone at some point. It can stem from various sources such as work, relationships, finances, or health concerns. While stress is a natural response to challenging situations, chronic stress can have detrimental effects on both our physical and mental well-being. Therefore, it is essential to have effective stress management techniques in place to help alleviate and prevent the negative impacts of stress.

One of the most effective stress management techniques is practicing mindfulness and relaxation exercises. Mindfulness involves focusing on the present moment and fully engaging with what you are doing, rather than dwelling on past events or worrying about the future. This can help reduce stress by calming the mind and promoting a sense of peace and relaxation. Relaxation exercises, such as deep breathing, progressive muscle relaxation, or guided imagery, can also help reduce stress by promoting physical and mental relaxation. These techniques can be practiced regularly to help manage stress and improve overall well-being.

Another effective stress management technique is engaging in regular physical activity. Exercise has been shown to have numerous benefits for both physical and mental health, including reducing stress levels. Physical activity releases endorphins, which are hormones that act as natural painkillers and mood elevators. Exercise also helps to reduce the levels of stress hormones, such as cortisol, in the body. Regular exercise can help improve mood, increase energy levels, and promote better sleep, all of which can help reduce stress and improve overall well-being.

In addition to mindfulness, relaxation exercises, and exercise, maintaining a healthy lifestyle can also help manage stress. Eating a balanced diet, getting an adequate amount of sleep, and staying hydrated are essential components of a healthy lifestyle that can help reduce stress. Eating a diet rich in fruits, vegetables, whole grains, and lean proteins can help provide the nutrients your body needs to cope with stress. Adequate sleep is also crucial for managing stress, as lack of sleep can exacerbate stress levels and decrease overall well-being. Staying hydrated by drinking plenty of water can also help support your body's stress response.

Additionally, seeking social support can be an effective stress management technique. Connecting with friends, family, or a support group can help provide a sense of belonging, reduce feelings of isolation, and offer emotional support during times of stress. Talking to someone you trust about your stressors can help provide perspective and potentially offer solutions to manage stress more effectively.

Building a strong support system can help you navigate challenging situations and cope with stress in a healthy way.

Furthermore, setting boundaries and managing time effectively can also help reduce stress levels. Learning to say no to commitments that are overwhelming or not essential can help prevent feelings of stress and overload. Prioritizing tasks and setting realistic goals can also help manage time effectively and reduce feelings of being overwhelmed. Setting aside time for self-care activities, such as hobbies, relaxation, or socializing, can also help reduce stress and maintain overall well-being. By incorporating mindfulness, relaxation exercises, regular physical activity, maintaining a healthy lifestyle, seeking social support, setting boundaries, and managing time effectively, individuals can develop a comprehensive approach to managing stress. These techniques can help reduce stress levels, improve well-being, and promote a healthier, more balanced life. By incorporating these stress management techniques into your daily routine, you can better cope with stress and lead a more fulfilling and enjoyable life.

- Building resilience and coping skills

Resilience and coping skills are essential aspects of mental health and well-being, particularly in the face of adversity and challenges. Building resilience involves developing the ability to bounce back from difficult situations, adapt to change, and overcome obstacles. It also involves cultivating coping skills that help individuals manage stress, emotions, and difficult circumstances effectively. By enhancing resilience and coping skills, individuals can better navigate the ups and downs of life, maintain a positive outlook, and thrive in the face of adversity.

One key aspect of building resilience is developing a sense of self-awareness and self-efficacy. Self-awareness involves understanding one's own strengths, weaknesses, emotions, and motivations, while self-efficacy involves believing in one's ability to overcome challenges and achieve goals. By developing a strong sense of self-awareness and self-efficacy, individuals can better cope with stress and adversity, as they are more likely to believe in their ability to overcome obstacles and persevere in difficult situations. This can help individuals maintain a positive outlook, remain focused on their goals, and find solutions to problems more effectively.

Another important aspect of building resilience is developing strong social connections and support networks. Having a supportive network of family, friends, colleagues, or mentors can provide individuals with emotional support, encouragement, and practical help during difficult times. Social connections can also provide opportunities for individuals to share their feelings, experiences, and perspectives, which can help them gain new insights, coping strategies, and perspectives on their challenges. By building strong social connections and support networks, individuals can feel less isolated, more connected, and better able to cope with stress and adversity.

In addition to self-awareness and social connections, developing effective coping skills is essential for building resilience. Coping skills are strategies and techniques that individuals use to manage stress, emotions, and difficult situations. These skills can include problem-solving, assertiveness, relaxation techniques, mindfulness, time management, and social support seeking, among others. By developing a range of coping skills, individuals can better manage their emotions, thoughts, and behaviors in response to stress and adversity, which can help them remain calm, focused, and adaptable in difficult situations.

One effective coping skill for building resilience is cognitive restructuring. Cognitive restructuring involves identifying and challenging negative or irrational thoughts and beliefs that contribute to stress, anxiety, or depression. By learning to recognize and replace negative thoughts with more positive, realistic, and adaptive interpretations, individuals can change their emotional responses and behaviors in response to difficult situations. This can help individuals build a more positive outlook, improve their mood, and feel more in control of their emotions and reactions.

Another important coping skill for building resilience is emotion regulation. Emotion regulation involves recognizing, understanding, and managing one's own emotions in a healthy and productive way. By developing skills to identify and express emotions, regulate emotional arousal, and cope with intense feelings, individuals can better manage stress, interpersonal conflicts, and difficult situations. Emotion regulation can help individuals stay calm, focused, and adaptive in the face of challenges, which can improve their ability to cope effectively and bounce back from adversity.

Furthermore, building resilience and coping skills also involves cultivating a sense of optimism and hope. Optimism involves having a positive outlook, expecting positive outcomes, and believing in one's ability to overcome challenges. By maintaining a hopeful attitude and focusing on solutions rather than problems, individuals can build resilience, enhance their coping skills, and find creative ways to navigate difficult situations. Optimism can help individuals maintain a sense of motivation, persistence, and adaptability in the face of setbacks, which can help them bounce back from adversity and achieve their goals. By developing self-awareness, social connections, effective coping skills, cognitive restructuring, emotion regulation, optimism, and hope, individuals can better manage stress, overcome obstacles, adapt to change, and thrive in difficult situations. Building resilience and coping skills is a lifelong process that requires effort, practice, and persistence, but the benefits of enhanced resilience and coping skills are well worth the investment. By building resilience and coping skills, individuals can cultivate the strength, flexibility, and emotional intelligence needed to navigate life's ups and downs with grace, resilience, and optimism.

Chapter 16: Positive Youth Development

- STRENGTH-BASED APPROACHES to working with teenagers

Strength-based approaches to working with teenagers are becoming increasingly popular in the fields of social work, counseling, and education. This approach focuses on identifying and building upon the strengths and positive attributes of teenagers, rather than solely focusing on their problems and deficits. By emphasizing teenagers' strengths, practitioners can empower them to tap into their own potential and resources to navigate challenges and achieve their goals.

One of the key principles of strength-based approaches is the belief that teenagers possess unique strengths and abilities that can be leveraged to enhance their well-being and success. This perspective is rooted in the positive psychology movement, which highlights the importance of focusing on what is right with individuals, rather than what is wrong with them. By identifying and nurturing teenagers' strengths, practitioners can help them develop a sense of self-efficacy and resilience, which are crucial for overcoming obstacles and thriving in the face of adversity.

Strength-based approaches also emphasize the importance of building positive and supportive relationships with teenagers. By establishing a trusting and collaborative relationship, practitioners can create a safe and empowering space for teenagers to explore and develop their strengths. This relational aspect of strength-based approaches is particularly important for teenagers, who are in a critical stage of development and often in need of guidance and support as they navigate the challenges of adolescence.

In addition to focusing on strengths and relationships, strength-based approaches also emphasize the importance of fostering a strengths-based mindset among practitioners. This involves shifting from a deficit-based mindset, which focuses on problems and limitations, to a strengths-based mindset, which focuses on possibilities and potential. By adopting a strengths-based mindset, practitioners can adopt a more positive and optimistic perspective, which can in turn empower teenagers to see themselves in a more positive light and approach challenges with greater resilience and confidence.

One of the key benefits of strength-based approaches is that they can help teenagers develop a sense of agency and ownership over their own lives. By focusing on their strengths and abilities, teenagers can develop a greater sense of self-awareness and self-confidence, which can empower them to take control of their own destinies and make positive choices that align with their goals and values. This sense of agency is particularly important for teenagers, who are often navigating complex social, emotional, and developmental challenges as they transition from childhood to adulthood.

Strength-based approaches can also help teenagers develop important life skills and competencies that are crucial for success in school, work, and relationships. By identifying and building upon their strengths, teenagers can develop a range of social and emotional skills, such as resilience, self-regulation, and empathy, which are essential for navigating the complexities of adolescence and building healthy and fulfilling relationships with others. These skills can also help teenagers develop a sense of purpose and direction in their lives, which can guide them towards positive and meaningful goals. By focusing on their strengths, building positive relationships, fostering a strengths-based mindset, and helping them develop a sense of agency and life skills, practitioners can empower teenagers to tap into their own potential and resources to overcome challenges and achieve their goals. Ultimately, strength-based approaches can help teenagers develop a sense of self-efficacy, resilience, and purpose, which are essential for thriving in adolescence and beyond.

- Empowerment and self-advocacy

Empowerment and self-advocacy are key concepts in promoting personal growth, self-confidence, and independence. Empowerment is the process of gaining the knowledge, skills, and resources necessary to make informed decisions and take control of one's life. It involves understanding your strengths and weaknesses, setting goals for yourself, and working towards achieving those goals. Self-advocacy, on the other hand, is the ability to speak up for yourself, assert your needs, and make your voice heard. It is about being your own best advocate and standing up for what you believe in.

Empowerment and self-advocacy go hand in hand. When you feel empowered, you are more likely to advocate for yourself and assert your rights. Likewise, when you practice self-advocacy, you become more empowered by taking ownership of your choices and actions. Together, these two concepts can help you navigate challenges, overcome obstacles, and achieve your full potential.

There are many ways to cultivate empowerment and practice self-advocacy in your daily life. One of the first steps is to develop a strong sense of self-awareness. This means understanding your values, beliefs, and priorities, as well as recognizing your own strengths and weaknesses. By knowing yourself well, you can make more informed decisions and stand up for what is important to you.

Another important aspect of empowerment and self-advocacy is building resilience. Life is full of ups and downs, and it is essential to develop the ability to bounce back from setbacks and overcome challenges. Resilience involves being flexible, adaptive, and persistent in the face of adversity. By building resilience, you can empower yourself to face obstacles head-on and keep moving forward towards your goals.

Communication is also a crucial skill in practicing self-advocacy. Effective communication involves expressing your thoughts, feelings, and needs clearly and confidently. This includes being able to listen actively, assert your boundaries, and negotiate for what you want. By honing your communication skills, you can advocate for yourself more effectively and build stronger relationships with others.

Self-care is another important aspect of empowerment and self-advocacy. Taking care of yourself physically, mentally, and emotionally is essential for maintaining your well-being and resilience. This includes getting enough rest, eating well, exercising regularly, and seeking help when needed. By prioritizing self-care, you can build the strength and energy needed to advocate for yourself and pursue your goals. By cultivating empowerment, building resilience, honing communication skills, and practicing self-care, you can empower yourself to take control of your life, assert your needs, and achieve your full potential. By embracing these concepts and incorporating them into your daily life, you can become your own best advocate and create a life that is fulfilling, meaningful, and empowered.

- Opportunities for personal growth and success

Personal growth and success are key pillars in leading a fulfilling and meaningful life. In today's fast-paced and competitive world, it is essential for individuals to continuously seek out opportunities for growth and development in order to reach their full potential. Opportunities for personal growth and success can come in various forms, such as educational pursuits, career advancement, personal development workshops, networking events, and self-reflection exercises. By actively engaging in these opportunities, individuals can enhance their skills, expand their knowledge base, and broaden their perspectives, ultimately leading to greater personal fulfillment and success.

One important avenue for personal growth and success is through education. By pursuing further education or acquiring new skills, individuals can enhance their knowledge base and expand their capabilities, opening up new opportunities for career advancement and personal development. Whether it be through traditional academic programs, online courses, or workshops and seminars, education plays a crucial role in personal growth and success. By investing in education, individuals not only acquire valuable skills and knowledge, but also demonstrate their commitment to self-improvement and lifelong learning.

In addition to formal education, career advancement is another key opportunity for personal growth and success. By setting ambitious career goals, seeking out new challenges, and actively pursuing opportunities for advancement, individuals can propel themselves forward in their careers and achieve greater levels of success. This may involve taking on leadership roles, seeking out mentorship opportunities, or pursuing further training and certifications. By actively engaging in their careers and seeking out opportunities for growth, individuals can enhance their skills, expand their networks, and position themselves for long-term success and fulfillment.

Another important avenue for personal growth and success is through personal development workshops and seminars. These events offer individuals the opportunity to learn new skills, gain valuable insights, and connect with like-minded individuals who are also committed to personal growth and development. Whether it be workshops focused on leadership skills, communication techniques, or mindfulness practices, personal development events can provide individuals with the tools and resources they need to enhance their personal and professional lives. By actively participating in these events, individuals can gain new perspectives, develop new skills, and build relationships that can support their growth and success.

Networking events also offer valuable opportunities for personal growth and success. By attending networking events, individuals can connect with professionals in their field, learn about new opportunities, and expand their networks. Networking events provide individuals with the chance to exchange ideas, gain valuable insights, and access new resources that can support their personal and professional growth. By actively engaging in networking events, individuals can enhance their visibility, build valuable relationships, and position themselves for future success and advancement.

Self-reflection exercises are another important avenue for personal growth and success. By taking the time to reflect on their goals, values, and priorities, individuals can gain valuable insights into themselves and identify areas for growth and improvement. Self-reflection exercises can involve journaling, meditation, or therapy sessions, all of which can help individuals gain a deeper understanding of themselves and their goals. By actively engaging in self-reflection exercises, individuals can cultivate self-awareness, clarify their values, and develop a clear vision for their future, ultimately leading to greater personal growth and success. By actively pursuing opportunities for education, career advancement, personal development, networking, and self-reflection, individuals can enhance their skills, expand their knowledge base, and broaden their perspectives, ultimately leading to greater personal fulfillment and success. By investing in their personal growth and development, individuals can position themselves for long-term success and fulfillment in both their personal and professional lives.

Chapter 17: Peer Mentoring and Support

- PEER MENTORING PROGRAMS and initiatives

Peer mentoring programs and initiatives play a vital role in promoting academic success and personal development among students. These programs provide valuable opportunities for students to connect with their peers, receive guidance and support, and develop important skills such as communication, leadership, and problem-solving. Peer mentoring relationships are characterized by mutual respect, trust, and collaboration, creating a positive and empowering environment for both mentors and mentees.

One of the key benefits of peer mentoring programs is the opportunity for mentees to receive personalized support and guidance from someone who has been in their shoes. Mentors can share their own experiences, insights, and strategies for success, helping mentees navigate academic challenges, set goals, and make informed decisions about their education and future career paths. By offering a unique perspective and serving as a role model, mentors can inspire and motivate mentees to achieve their full potential and overcome obstacles they may face along the way.

In addition to academic support, peer mentoring programs also promote social and emotional growth among students. Mentors can offer a listening ear, provide emotional support, and help mentees build confidence, self-esteem, and resilience. By fostering positive relationships and a sense of belonging, peer mentoring programs contribute to a supportive and inclusive campus community where students feel valued, understood, and empowered to succeed.

Furthermore, peer mentoring programs serve as a valuable supplement to formal academic advising and support services offered by colleges and universities. While advisors play a critical role in helping students navigate academic requirements and develop academic plans, mentors can provide a more personalized and informal approach to mentoring that complements the formal advising process. Mentors can offer additional insights, resources, and support that may not be readily available through traditional advising channels, creating a more holistic and comprehensive support system for students.

Moreover, peer mentoring programs are not only beneficial for mentees but also for mentors themselves. Mentors gain valuable leadership, communication, and interpersonal skills through their mentoring experience, which can enhance their own personal and professional development. By serving as mentors, students have the opportunity to give back to their community, make a positive impact on their peers, and develop a sense of responsibility and accountability for supporting the success of others. This reciprocal relationship between mentors and mentees fosters a culture of collaboration, teamwork, and mutual respect that benefits all participants involved in the program.

In order to ensure the effectiveness and sustainability of peer mentoring programs, institutions must invest in training, resources, and support for both mentors and mentees. Training programs should focus on building mentorship skills, fostering effective communication and rapport-building, and promoting cultural competence and diversity awareness. Institutions should also provide mentors and mentees with ongoing support, feedback, and opportunities for reflection and growth to enhance the quality and impact of the mentoring experience. By fostering positive relationships, offering personalized support, and promoting academic and social growth, peer mentoring programs contribute to a supportive and inclusive learning environment where students can thrive and reach their full potential. With the right resources, training, and support in place, institutions can create a vibrant and effective peer mentoring program that benefits both mentors and mentees and enhances the overall student experience.

- Creating a supportive peer network

Creating a supportive peer network is essential for personal and professional growth. Having a network of peers who share similar interests and goals can provide valuable support, feedback, and encouragement. Whether you are a student looking for study buddies, an entrepreneur seeking advice from other business owners, or a professional seeking opportunities for collaboration and mentorship, a supportive peer network can be a valuable resource. In this article, we will explore the benefits of creating a supportive peer network, as well as some practical tips for building and maintaining strong connections with your peers.

One of the key benefits of having a supportive peer network is the opportunity to exchange ideas and receive feedback from others who share your interests and goals. By surrounding yourself with like-minded individuals, you can gain fresh perspectives on your work, receive constructive criticism, and brainstorm new ideas. This can be particularly valuable for students seeking study partners, entrepreneurs looking for feedback on their business ideas, or professionals seeking advice on career development or project management. A supportive peer network can help you expand your knowledge and skills, challenge your assumptions, and push you to achieve greater success.

Another benefit of creating a supportive peer network is the opportunity for collaboration and mutual support. By building relationships with your peers, you can access a wealth of resources and expertise that can help you overcome challenges and achieve your goals. Whether you are looking for a business partner, a mentor, or simply a friend to bounce ideas off of, a supportive peer network can provide the support and encouragement you need to succeed. Collaborating with your peers can also help you build strong relationships and establish a sense of community, which can be invaluable for boosting your confidence and motivation.

In addition to providing valuable feedback and support, a supportive peer network can also help you expand your professional network and access new opportunities. By building strong relationships with your peers, you can tap into their networks and connections, which can open up new doors for collaboration, mentorship, and career advancement. Attending networking events, conferences, and workshops with your peers can also help you expand your circle of contacts, leading to new job opportunities, partnerships, and collaborations. By actively participating in your peer network and supporting others in their goals, you can position yourself as a valuable member of the community and attract new opportunities and relationships.

So, how can you go about creating a supportive peer network. One of the first steps is to identify individuals who share your interests and goals. This could involve reaching out to classmates, colleagues, or fellow professionals in your field, or joining online communities and forums dedicated to your area of interest. By actively participating in these groups and engaging with other members, you can start building relationships and establishing connections with like-minded individuals. Once you have identified potential peers, make an effort to engage with them on a regular basis, whether through social media, email, or in-person meetings. By staying in touch and offering support and encouragement, you can start to build strong relationships that will form the foundation of your peer network.

Another important aspect of creating a supportive peer network is to be willing to give as much as you receive. Building strong connections with your peers requires a willingness to offer support, feedback, and encouragement in return. By actively participating in group discussions, sharing your own expertise and insights, and offering help and advice to others, you can demonstrate your value as a member of the community and strengthen your relationships with your peers. Remember, a supportive peer network is a two-way street, so make an effort to contribute as much as you can and be generous with your time and resources. By surrounding yourself with like-minded individuals who share your interests and goals, you can gain valuable feedback, support, and collaboration opportunities that can help you achieve greater success. By actively participating in your peer network, offering support and encouragement to others, and being open to new ideas and perspectives, you can build strong relationships that will enrich your life and help you reach your full potential. So take the time to invest in building and maintaining your peer network – the benefits are boundless.

- Peer-to-peer support for mental health and well-being

Peer-to-peer support for mental health and well-being is a crucial component of the mental health landscape. It involves individuals with lived experience of mental health challenges providing support to others who may be going through similar struggles. This form of support is based on the principle of shared understanding and empathy, which can create a safe space for individuals to feel heard, validated, and understood. Peer support offers a unique perspective that professionals may not always be able to provide, as peers can offer firsthand knowledge and insights that come from their own journeys of recovery and resilience.

One of the key benefits of peer-to-peer support for mental health is the sense of connection and belonging that it can foster. Many individuals who are struggling with mental health issues may feel isolated and alone, but connecting with peers who understand what they are going through can provide a sense of camaraderie and solidarity. This can help to combat feelings of shame and stigma, which are often associated with mental health challenges. By sharing their own stories and experiences, peers can validate the struggles of others and offer hope and encouragement for recovery and healing.

In addition to the emotional support that peer-to-peer support provides, it can also be a valuable source of practical assistance and guidance. Peers can offer tips and strategies for coping with symptoms, navigating the healthcare system, and accessing resources for treatment and support. They can also serve as role models for recovery, demonstrating that it is possible to overcome mental health challenges and live a fulfilling and meaningful life. By sharing their own successes and setbacks, peers can inspire others to take control of their own mental health and well-being.

Another important aspect of peer-to-peer support for mental health is its potential to empower individuals to become advocates for themselves and others. By participating in peer support groups or peer mentoring programs, individuals can develop skills in active listening, empathy, and communication, which can be valuable in their personal and professional lives. They can also become more knowledgeable about mental health issues and ways to promote mental well-being, which can help to reduce the stigma surrounding mental illness and encourage others to seek help when needed. In this way, peer support can have a ripple effect, leading to positive changes within communities and society as a whole.

It is important to note that peer support is not a replacement for professional mental health treatment, but rather a complementary and supplemental form of support. Peers are not trained therapists or counselors, and they should not be expected to provide clinical interventions or medical advice. However, they can play a valuable role in enhancing the overall treatment and support that individuals receive, by offering a unique perspective and understanding that may not be present in traditional mental health services. By working in collaboration with mental health professionals, peers can help to create a more holistic and person-centered approach to mental health care. By sharing their own experiences, insights, and resources, peers can create a sense of connection and understanding that is essential for healing and growth. Peer support can help to combat feelings of isolation and stigma, provide practical assistance and guidance, empower individuals to become advocates for themselves and others, and enhance the overall quality of mental health care. By recognizing the importance of peer support and incorporating it into mental health services, we can create a more inclusive, supportive, and effective system of care for all individuals who are dealing with mental health issues.

Chapter 18: Conclusion

- RECAP OF KEY CONCEPTS and strategies

In order to fully understand and implement key concepts and strategies, it is important to first recap and review the fundamental principles that underlie successful practices in any field. Key concepts are the foundational ideas that guide our actions and decisions, while strategies are the specific approaches we use to achieve our goals. By mastering these concepts and strategies, individuals can improve their performance, decision-making, and overall success.

One key concept to keep in mind is the importance of goal-setting. Setting clear, specific, and achievable goals helps individuals to focus their energy and resources towards a desired outcome. Without clear goals, individuals may find themselves moving in a directionless manner, without a defined purpose or objective. By setting goals, individuals can prioritize their efforts and work towards tangible results.

Another important concept to consider is the power of self-awareness. Understanding one's strengths, weaknesses, motivations, and values is essential for personal growth and development. Self-awareness allows individuals to make informed decisions, capitalize on their strengths, and address their weaknesses. By honing in on self-awareness, individuals can cultivate a sense of authenticity and confidence that will enhance their performance and effectiveness.

Additionally, the concept of resilience is key in navigating challenges and setbacks. Resilience refers to the ability to bounce back from difficult situations, adapt to change, and persevere in the face of adversity. It is a crucial skill to develop, as it allows individuals to maintain a positive mindset, stay focused on their goals, and overcome obstacles with determination and resolve.

When it comes to strategies, one effective approach is to leverage one's strengths and talents. By identifying and utilizing their areas of expertise, individuals can maximize their impact and achieve success more efficiently. This strategy involves focusing on what one does best, rather than trying to be proficient in every area. By playing to their strengths, individuals can position themselves for success and stand out in their field.

Another valuable strategy is to cultivate a growth mindset. A growth mindset is the belief that abilities and talents can be developed through hard work, dedication, and perseverance. By adopting this mindset, individuals can embrace challenges, learn from failures, and continually strive for improvement. This strategy fosters a sense of resilience, adaptability, and a commitment to lifelong learning.

Furthermore, effective communication is a key strategy for success in any endeavor. Clear, concise, and persuasive communication is essential for building relationships, fostering collaboration, and achieving desired outcomes. By honing their communication skills, individuals can convey their ideas effectively, build trust with others, and navigate conflicts with diplomacy and tact. By understanding and applying fundamental principles, individuals can enhance their performance, decision-making, and overall effectiveness. By setting goals, cultivating self-awareness, building resilience, leveraging strengths, fostering a growth mindset, and honing communication skills, individuals can position themselves for success and achieve their desired outcomes. Implementing these key concepts and strategies will not only lead to personal growth and development but also contribute to professional advancement and success.

- Encouragement for continued learning and growth

Continued learning and growth are essential elements of personal and professional development. In today's fast-paced and ever-changing world, it is crucial for individuals to continuously expand their knowledge and skills in order to stay relevant and competitive. Whether in the workplace or in everyday life, the pursuit of learning should be a priority for everyone.

One of the key benefits of continued learning is the opportunity to acquire new knowledge and skills that can help individuals advance in their careers. By staying up-to-date on the latest trends and developments in their field, individuals can position themselves as valuable assets to their employers and increase their chances of career growth and advancement. Additionally, learning new skills can open up new opportunities for individuals, enabling them to explore different career paths and pursue their passions.

Continued learning also plays a crucial role in personal growth and development. By challenging themselves to learn new things, individuals can expand their horizons, broaden their perspectives, and enhance their problem-solving abilities. Learning can also boost confidence and self-esteem, as individuals gain a sense of accomplishment and fulfillment from mastering new skills and knowledge. In essence, continued learning can help individuals become more well-rounded and adaptable individuals, better equipped to navigate the complexities of modern life.

It is important for individuals to cultivate a mindset of lifelong learning in order to fully realize their potential. This mindset involves being open to new ideas, seeking out opportunities for growth, and embracing challenges as opportunities for personal and professional development. By approaching learning with a positive and curious attitude, individuals can overcome obstacles and setbacks, and ultimately achieve their goals and aspirations.

One of the key factors that can help individuals stay motivated and committed to continued learning is setting clear goals and objectives. By establishing specific targets and milestones, individuals can track their progress and measure their success, which can in turn boost motivation and drive. Additionally, setting goals can help individuals stay focused and prioritize their learning efforts, ensuring that they are making progress towards their desired outcomes.

Another important aspect of continued learning is seeking out feedback and guidance from mentors and peers. By soliciting input from others, individuals can gain valuable insights and perspectives that can help them identify areas for improvement and make informed decisions about their learning journey. Mentors can provide valuable advice and support, while peers can offer encouragement and accountability, helping individuals stay motivated and focused on their learning goals. By embracing a mindset of lifelong learning, setting clear goals, seeking feedback, and staying motivated, individuals can expand their knowledge and skills, advance their careers, and achieve their full potential. In today's fast-paced and ever-changing world, the pursuit of learning should be a priority for everyone, as it can open up new opportunities, enrich lives, and empower individuals to become the best versions of themselves.

- **Resources for further support and information**

When seeking further support and information, it is crucial to utilize a variety of resources to ensure thorough understanding and accurate knowledge. Whether you are conducting research for an academic paper, seeking guidance on a specific topic, or looking for professional development opportunities, there are numerous avenues available to access additional support and information.

One of the most common resources for further support and information is academic libraries. These institutions typically have vast collections of books, journals, and other materials that can provide valuable insights and data on a wide range of topics. Librarians are also excellent resources themselves, as they are trained to assist with research inquiries and can help guide you in the right direction. Additionally, many academic libraries offer access to online databases and academic journals, which can be invaluable for finding up-to-date information and research studies.

Another valuable resource for further support and information is academic conferences and workshops. These events bring together experts in various fields to discuss current research, trends, and best practices. Attending these conferences can provide you with the opportunity to network with other professionals, learn from experts in the field, and gain new insights into your area of interest. Many conferences also offer workshops and seminars on specific topics, allowing you to delve deeper into a particular subject area.

Online resources are also a valuable tool for accessing further support and information. Websites such as Google Scholar, ResearchGate, and academia. edu provide access to millions of academic articles, research studies, and scholarly papers. These platforms can be particularly useful for conducting literature reviews, accessing primary sources, and staying updated on the latest research in your field. Additionally, many universities and research institutions have their own online repositories where you can access research publications and reports.

Professional organizations and associations are another valuable resource for further support and information. These groups typically offer a wealth of resources, including publications, webinars, conferences, and networking opportunities. Joining a professional organization can provide you with access to a community of like-minded professionals who can offer support, guidance, and mentorship. Many professional organizations also offer certification programs, continuing education courses, and job boards, allowing you to enhance your skills and advance your career.

Lastly, social media platforms can be a valuable resource for accessing further support and information. Platforms such as LinkedIn, Twitter, and Facebook can connect you with experts in your field, allow you to join professional groups and forums, and provide opportunities for networking and collaboration. Many professionals share articles, research studies, and insights on social media, making it a valuable tool for staying informed and connected with the latest trends and developments in your field. By utilizing a combination of academic libraries, conferences, online resources, professional organizations, and social media platforms, you can enhance your knowledge, network with other professionals, and stay informed on the latest developments in your field. Remember to approach these resources with curiosity and an open mind, as they can provide valuable insights and opportunities for growth and learning.

www.ingramcontent.com/pod-product-compliance
Lightning Source LLC
Chambersburg PA
CBHW071918120726
48001CB00005B/1777